AF395683

Ashley Jackson's *Watercolour Sketches*

Ashley Jackson's *Watercolour Sketches*

Ashley Jackson

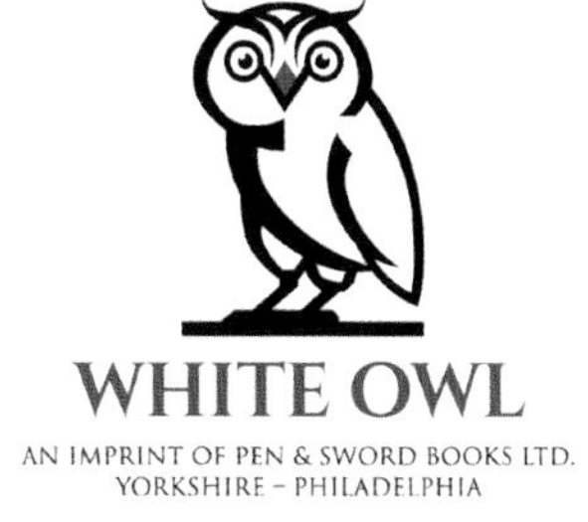

WHITE OWL

AN IMPRINT OF PEN & SWORD BOOKS LTD.
YORKSHIRE – PHILADELPHIA

First published in Great Britain in 2019 by
White Owl Books
An imprint of
Pen & Sword Books Ltd
Yorkshire - Philadelphia

ISBN 978 1 52674 424 1

A CIP catalogue record for this book is available from the British Library.

Printed and bound by Replika Press Pvt Ltd, India
Typeset by Aura Technology and Software Services, India

Pen & Sword Books Ltd incorporates the Imprints of Pen & Sword Books Archaeology, Atlas, Aviation, Battleground, Discovery, Family History, History, Maritime, Military, Naval, Politics, Railways, Select, Transport, True Crime, Fiction, Frontline Books, Leo Cooper, Praetorian Press, Seaforth Publishing, Wharncliffe and White Owl.

For a complete list of Pen & Sword titles please contact

PEN & SWORD BOOKS LIMITED
47 Church Street, Barnsley, South Yorkshire, S70 2AS, England
E-mail: enquiries@pen-and-sword.co.uk
Website: www.pen-and-sword.co.uk

or

PEN AND SWORD BOOKS
1950 Lawrence Rd, Havertown, PA 19083, USA
E-mail: uspen-and-sword@casematepublishers.com
Website: www.penandswordbooks.com

Contents

Dedication

To my daughter Claudia for all the help and dedication in bringing this book together and for her willingness to be there in all parts of my life.

Introduction

*To see the spirit of Yorkshire and its
moors through your eyes is one thing,
Many people look but only a few will
see and feel its very soul.*
(Ashley Jackson, 1970)

I wrote this in my sketchbook as a young man of thirty. Having studied the landscape for over fifty years, I still believe this comment to be true, but what I would like to do is encourage everyone to see the moors and natural landscapes.

If we are but guardians for the next generation, how do we teach them to have respect for something they see no value in? To me it is a feeling that you cannot put a price on. In a world of technological advances, virtual reality has its place, but as a self-confessed old timer I can honestly say that nothing to me compares to the reality of standing on those moors and just breathing it all in; experiencing first-hand the sights, the sounds, the raw emotion.

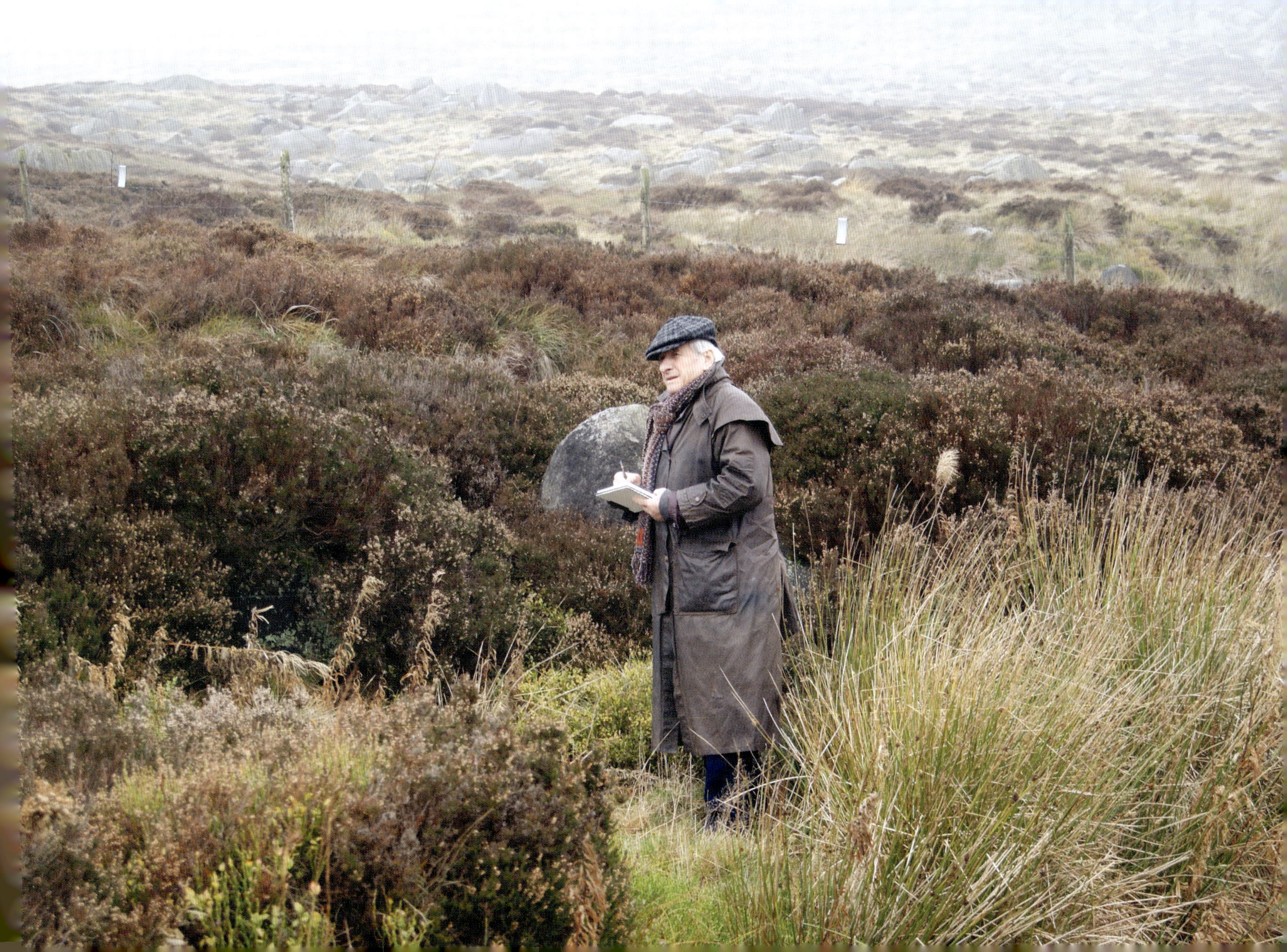

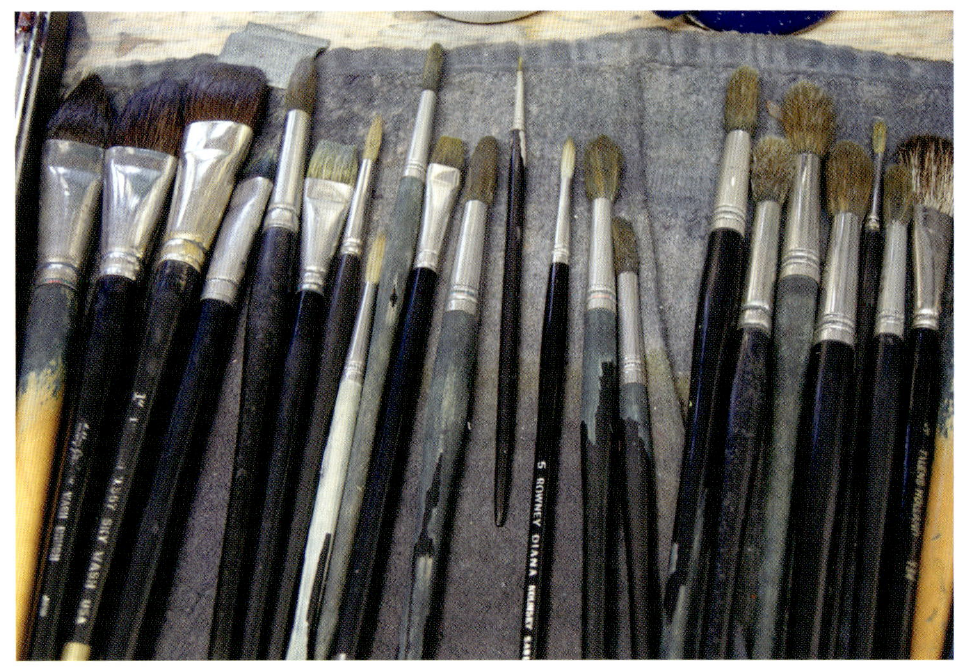

"I paint for myself. I don't know how to do anything else, anyway." Francis Bacon

I know I am fortunate to have made a living and raised my family by doing something I enjoyed. Painting has never been a job to me; it has been my life, and I truly do not know what else I would have done as I had no plan B.

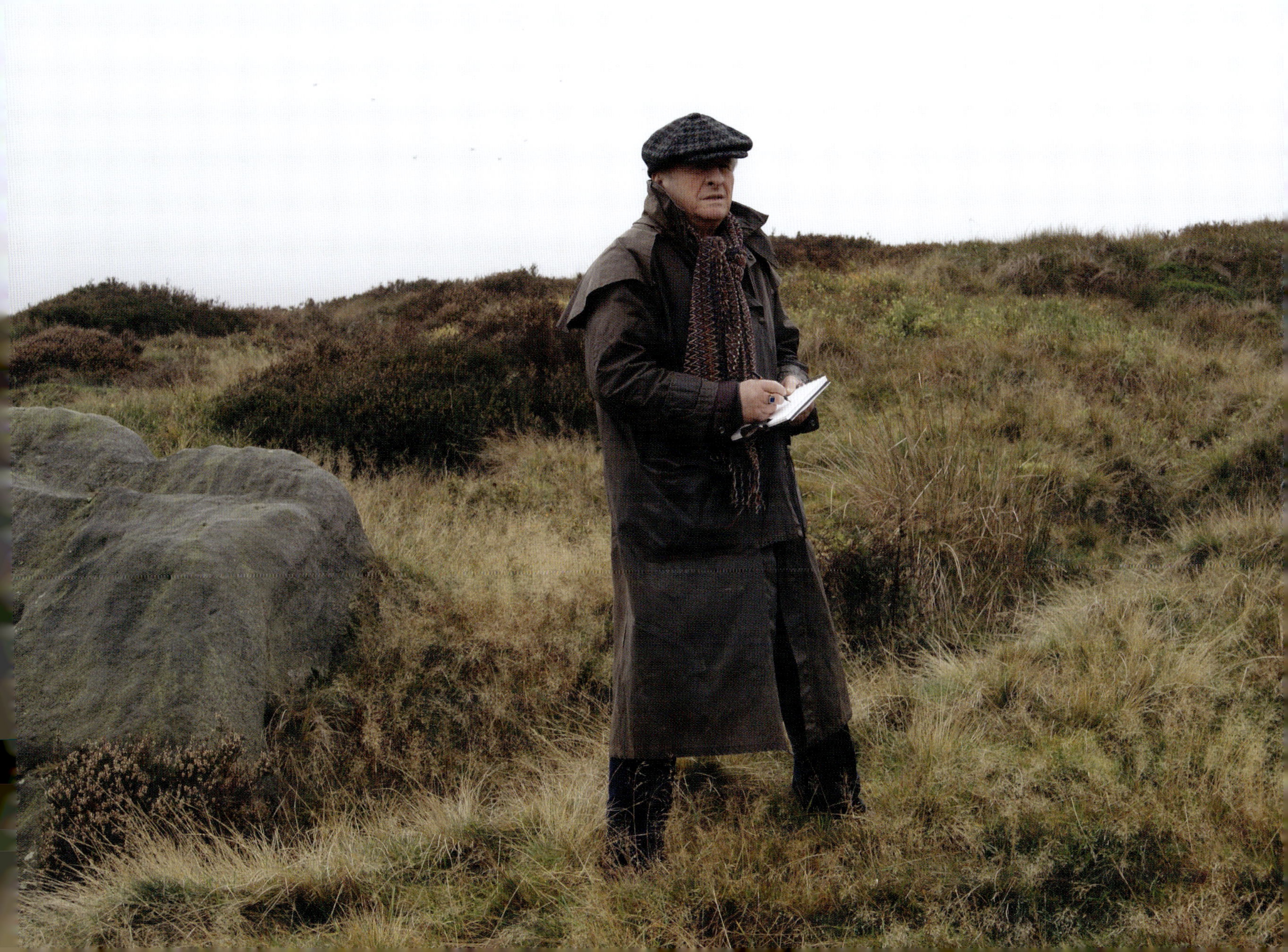

Hebden

Here I am at Hebden, a village within the parish of Craven, North Yorkshire. It is a designated conservation area within the Yorkshire Dales National Park due to its historic settlement patterns, and was first mentioned in the Doomsday book of 1086.

As I have often said, "Some days are diamond and some days are stone", but if you only venture out on the sunny days how will you ever know which days are which?

Thus although this sketch says it was 'raining again', I make no apology, for there is more drama in a rain-filled sky or impending storm than there is in a blue sky 'perfect' day.

A gold post box stands outside the old post office, commemorating the 2012 Olympic Games gold medal won by the rower Andrew Triggs Hodge, who grew up in the village.

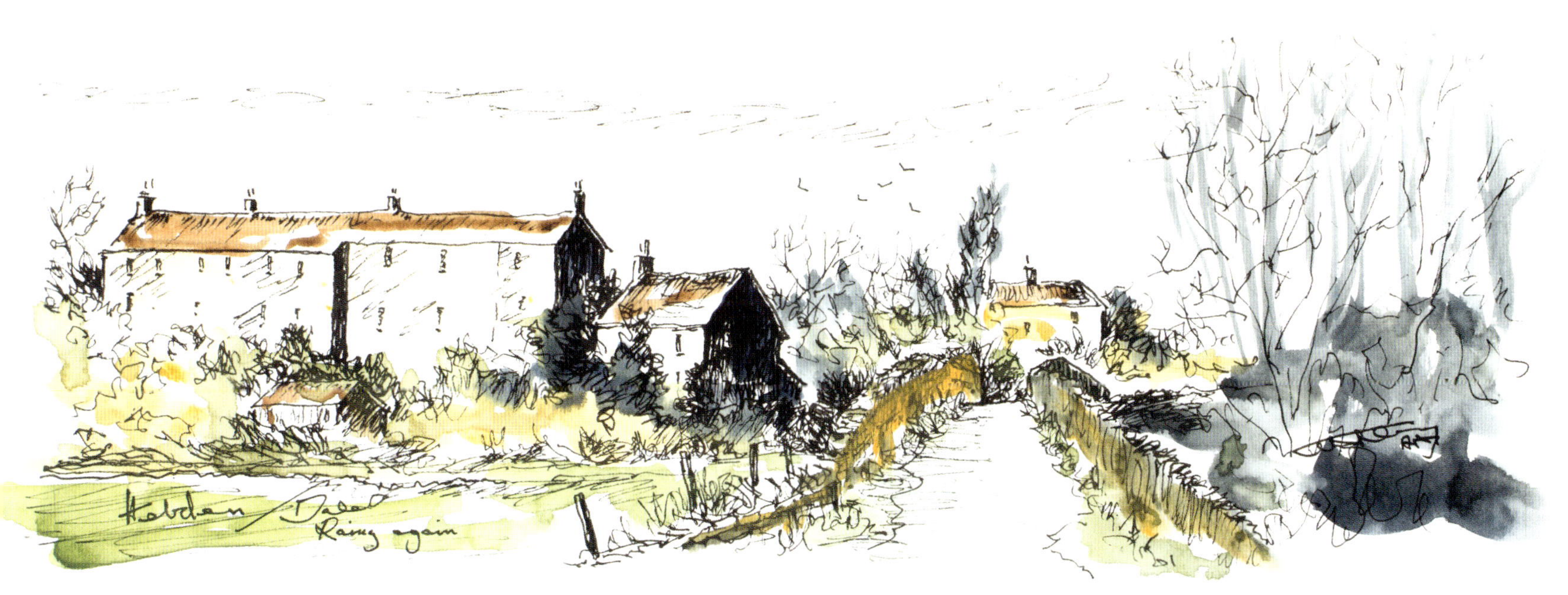

Hebden Dale
Raining again

Burnsall

Nestled in the valley amongst the trees along the River Wharfe, in Wharfedale, is the village of Burnsall, with its five-arched bridge and St. Wilfrid's Church in the background. It is probably one of the most popular villages to visit in the summer, with families taking picnics along the banks of the river. It is not far from Hebden and Appletreewick, which are also very much worth a visit.

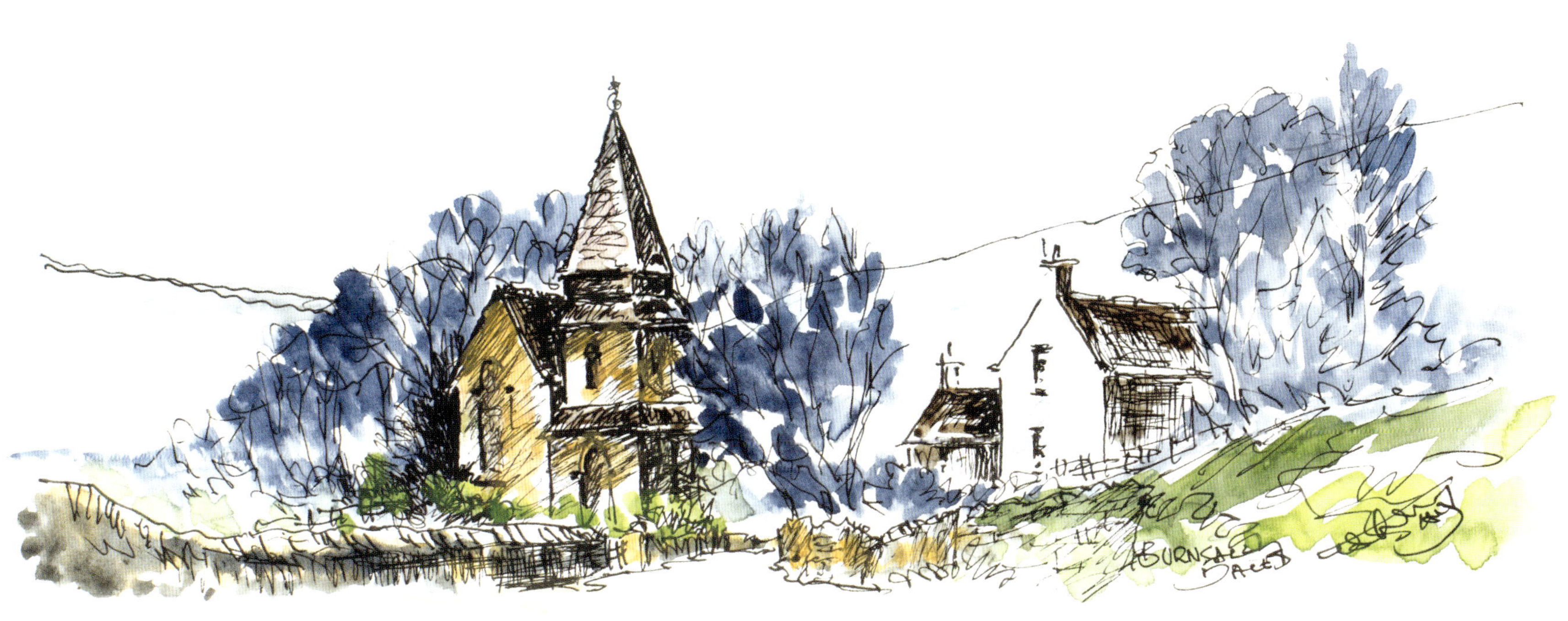

Looking to Simon's Seat

There appear to be many origins to the name 'Simon's Seat', the name given to this rocky outcrop that forms the summit of Barden Hill. The heather–clad moorland ascends up to the coarse sandstone summit, resulting in a spectacular panoramic view. Lying above Bolton Abbey, on the Duke of Devonshire's estate in Wharfedale, there are many walks to enjoy in this area, but be aware that the land is part of the Barden Moor access agreement, meaning dogs are not allowed, and there may be days when the moor is shut for shooting.

The nearby Valley of Desolation sounds as if it belongs in a black and white western, but is in fact named after a great storm in 1826. The truly wonderful forest is the result of an intervention to recreate the woodland that was lost in the storm.

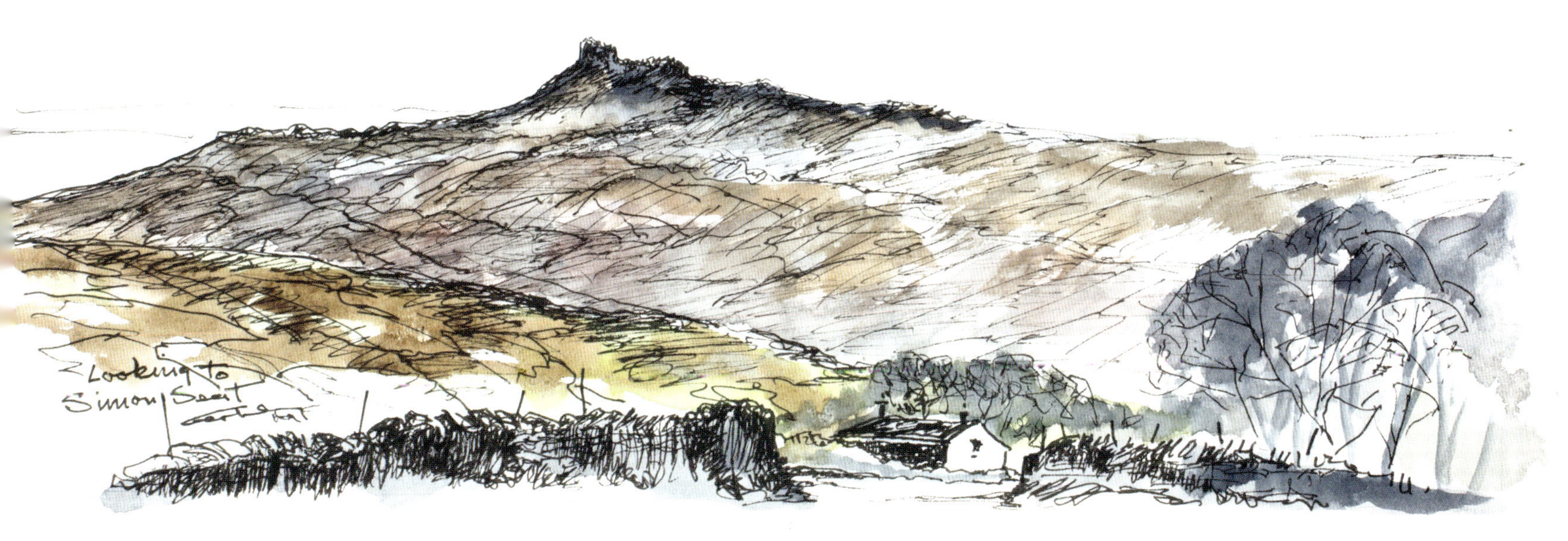

Looking to
Simon Seat

Langsett Moor and Reservoir

This really is a landscape of two halves; the first being the secluded walk alongside the reservoir edge, looking out across the water as if you have been transported to a Scottish glen, whilst on the other side of the water you experience a breathtaking open moorland that can only be Yorkshire.

Langsett has been my muse for many years through the sunshine and rain, but as you will know I prefer to capture the drama and atmosphere of the sky. So if you take the walk on a dark, thunderous day you might find a man and a sketch book crouched behind a dry stone wall ….. do say "hello".

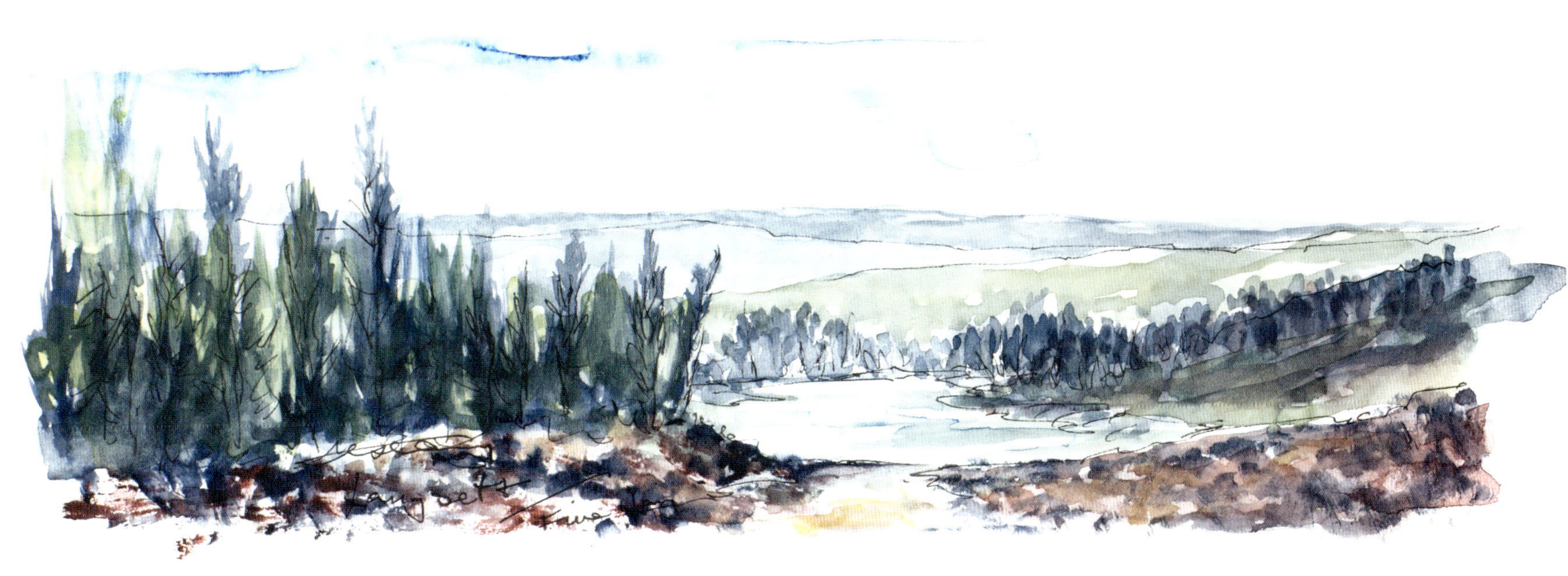

Langsett Moor and Res.
Midhope Moors.

Linton

I have fond memories of filming in Linton for my Yorkshire Television series, 'A Brush with Ashley', alongside my friend from Barnsley, Brian Glover, who was not only a good mate, but a humorous drinking partner. We would spend many a good hour with the writer, Willis Hall, and Neil Hodgkinson and Anne Pickles from the *Yorkshire Evening Post*. They were happy days. Needless to say there is a lovely pub in the village, and the additions of a stunning church and picturesque 'Little Emily's' bridge make it a great visiting destination.

If you look carefully at the sketch, and those throughout the book, you will see that alongside the drawing is often a description of the weather on that day.

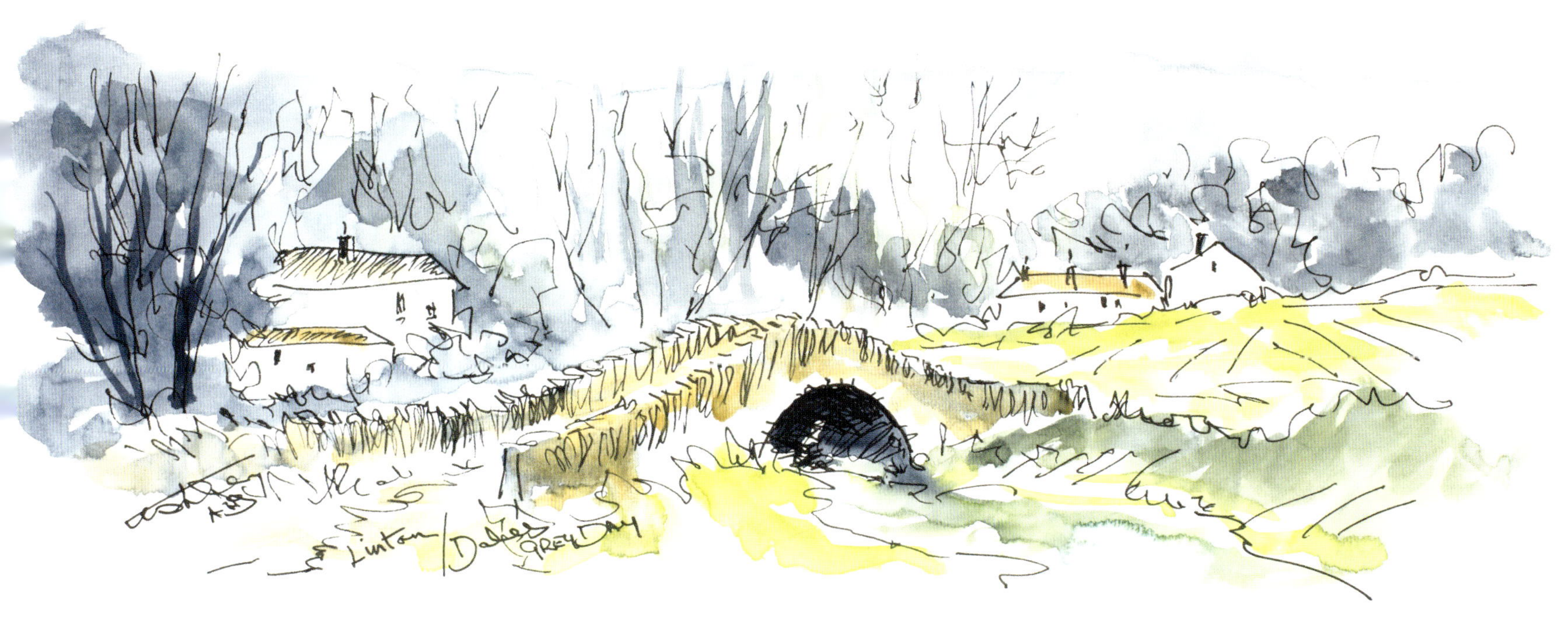

Linton/Dales GREY DAY

On the Way to Appletreewick

Just 12 miles from Skipton is the small village of Appletreewick. As I turned this corner my journey came to a stop as I wished to recreate the harmony of the Yorkshire Dales; man living in close contact with the moorland, woodland and the fell. It is not often that you get to capture a scene that requires no 'artistic licence', but this vista had everything.

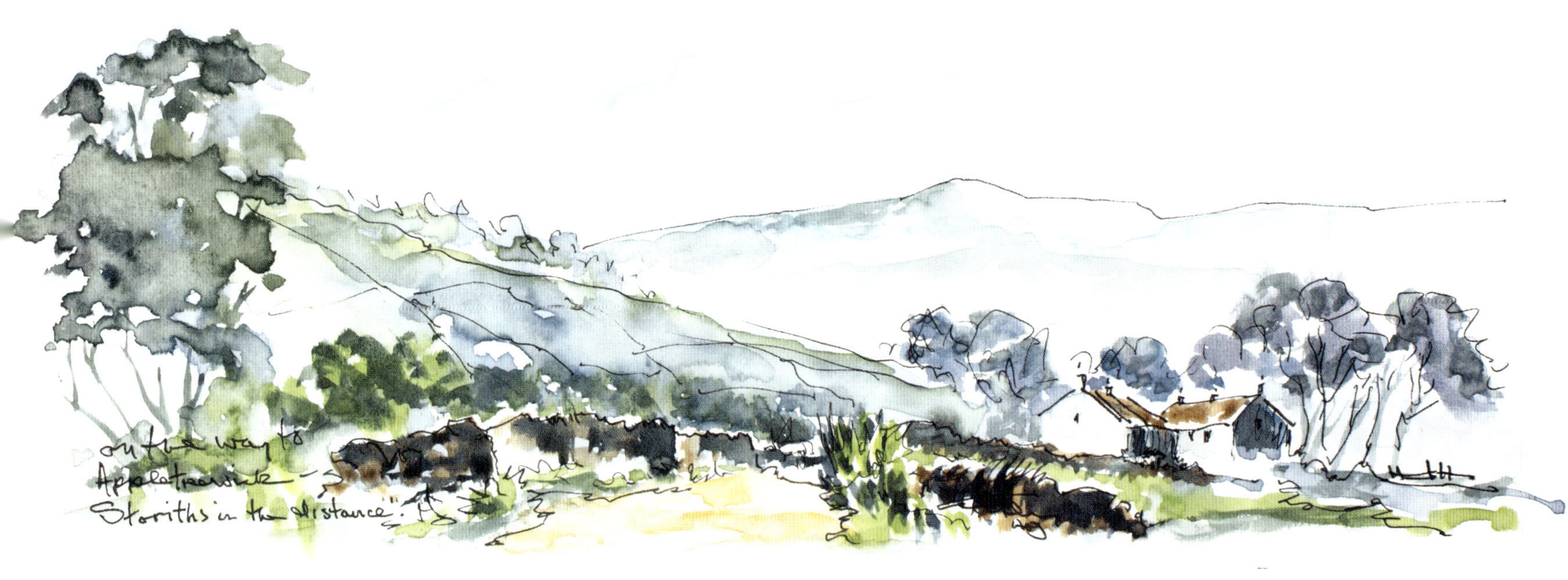

on the way to
Appletreewick —
Storiths in the distance".

Burnsall

Here I return to Burnsall to show you the complexity of the view from a distance; the five arched bridge, St Wilfred's Church and the landscape that surrounds the village. To quote JMW Turner, "There's a sketch at every turn" and for the Yorkshire Dales, this goes without saying.

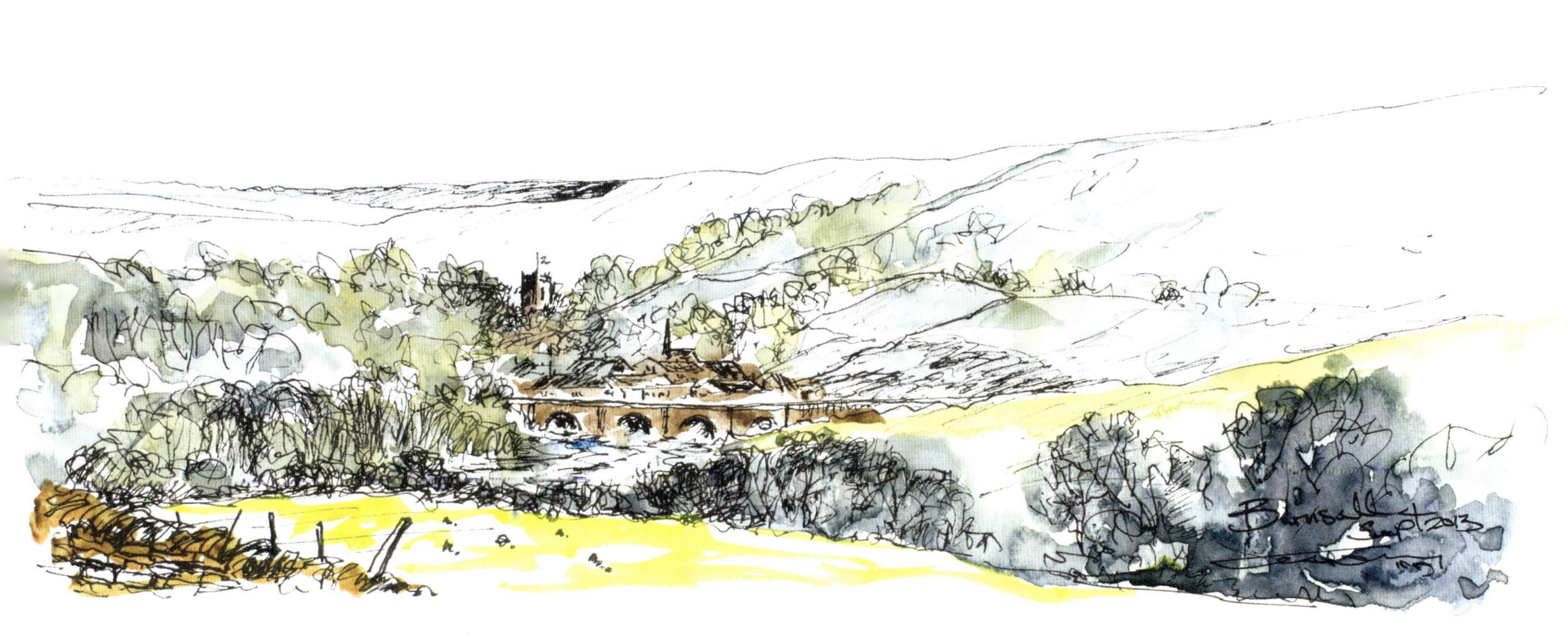

Roxby Beck, Staithes

Yorkshire has some fantastic coastal landscapes, but I have to admit to having a soft spot for Staithes. This was a crisp day, cold enough to need an extra layer or two of clothing. The funny thing is that when I'm inspired, I can stand and sketch all day without feeling the cold and on this occasion you could not fail to notice the vibrancy of the colours before me, hence it was with eagerness that I set about capturing the moment.

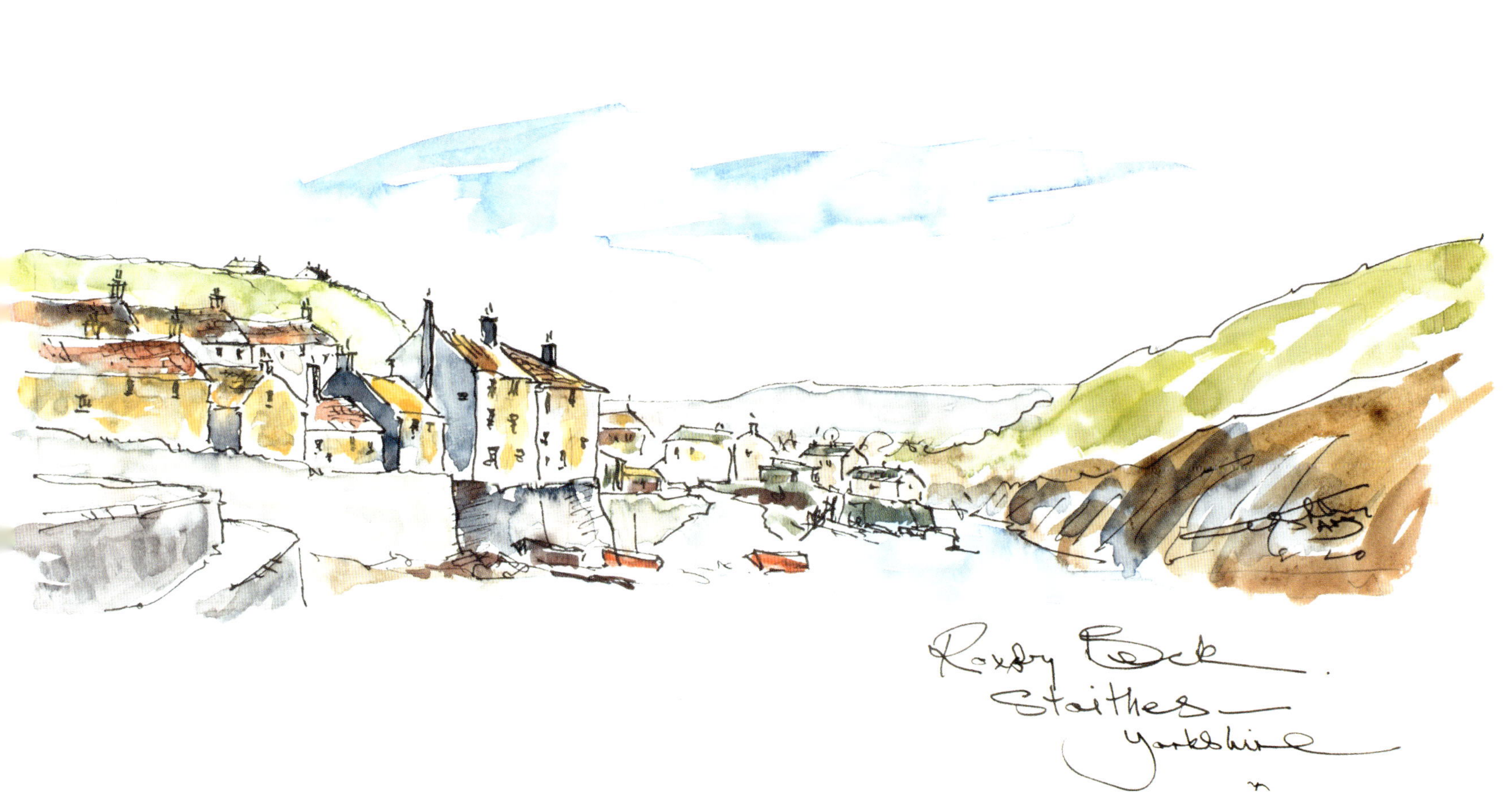

Roxby Beck
Staithes
Yorkshire

Looking Out to Sea from Roxby Beck

I was so inspired by the colours of Staithes that I was to take great pleasure in capturing it in more than one sketch. This one is heading out to sea with the seagulls appearing to dance across the sky.

"The richness I achieve comes from nature, the source of my inspiration." Monet

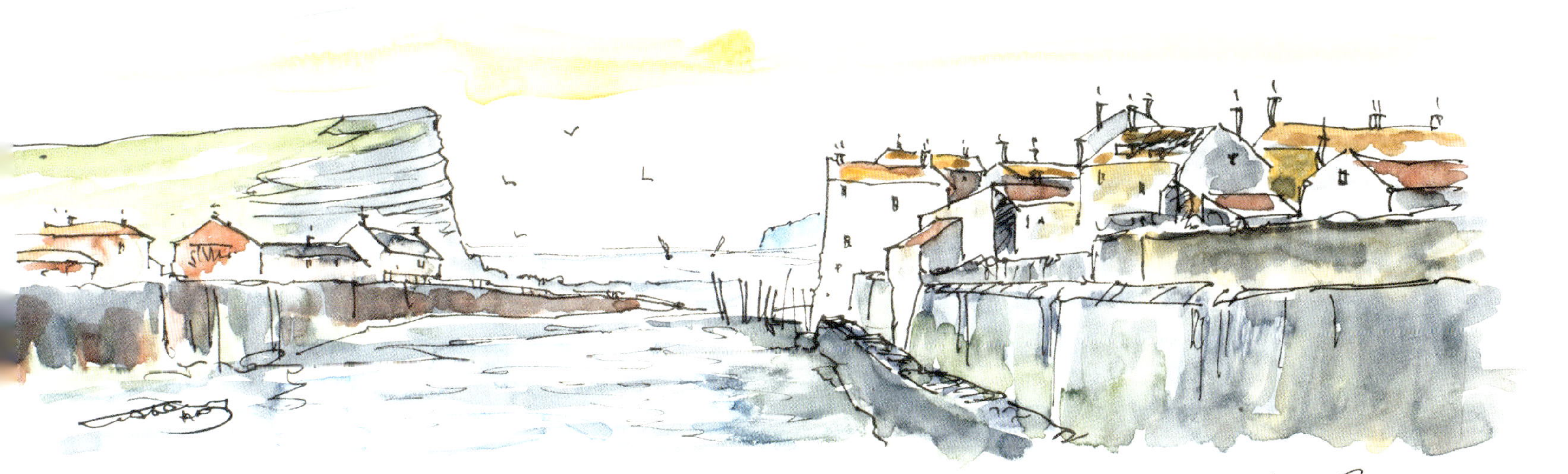

Looking out to Sea, from Roxby Beck
Staithes

Choppards and Castle Hill

This is one of my favourite landscapes close to home and I have undertaken many a paint day with students at the Mission, along the lane. It is quite exposed on this side of the valley and even in May you could be unsure of the weather and if it would be kind to us.

Working alongside Kirklees Council, a few years ago we produced a walk that includes this panorama, so visitors to Holmfirth can take in the hidden gems that surround us, and which might previously have been missed because they were not sign posted.

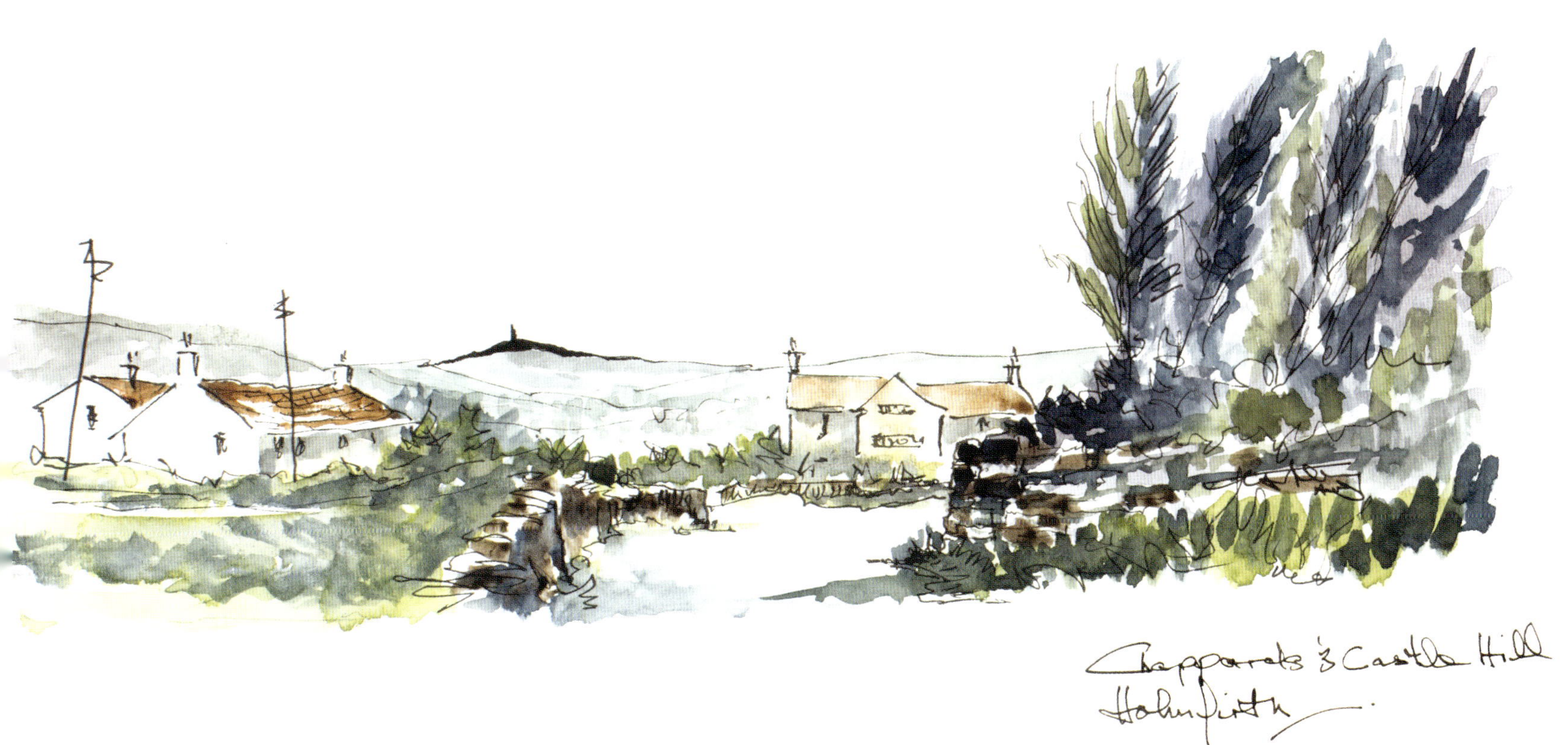

Choppards & Castle Hill
Holmfirth

Carperby

Carperby is a tranquil location near Castle Bolton. It is on the quieter side of Wensleydale and what I call the sunny side of the valley, enjoying as it does the sun for the majority of the day. It is a picturesque dale and was the honeymoon destination of Mr and Mrs Alf Wight, better known as James Herriot. If you are planning a visit Asygarth Falls, it is but a short stroll away and as us Yorkshire folk like a great deal, you would be getting 'two for the price of one' as destinations go.

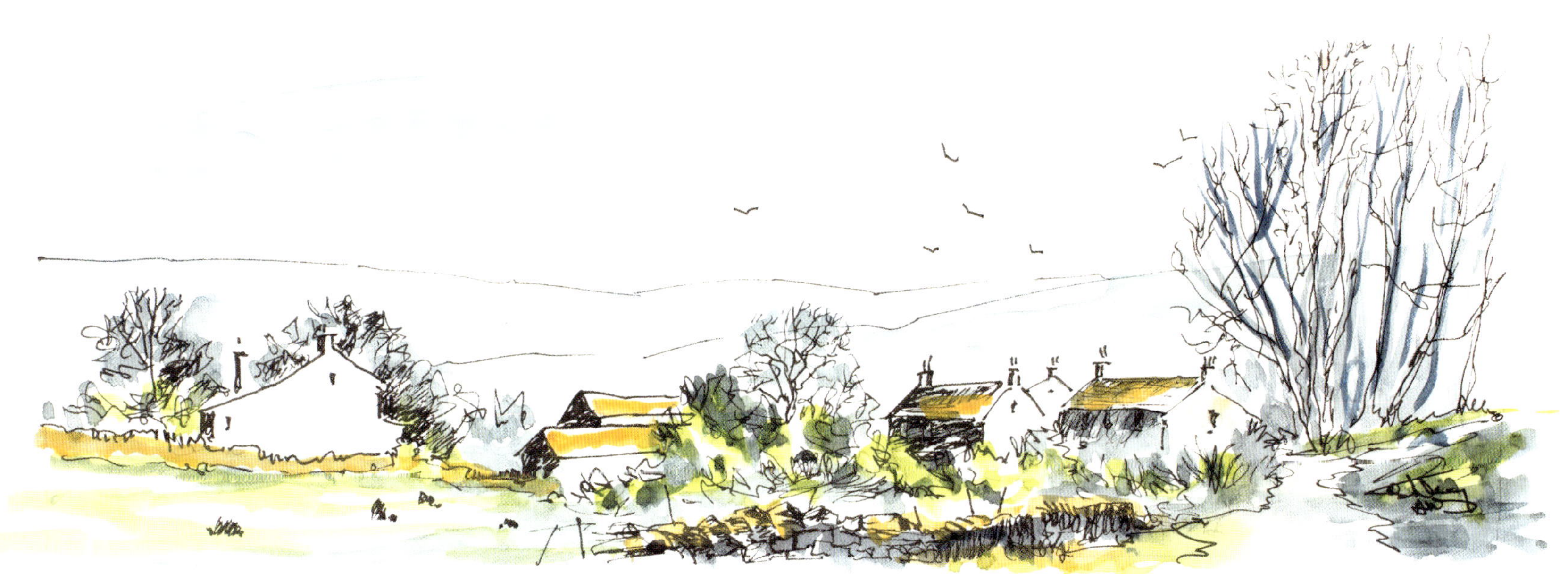

Carperby. Wensleydale.

Goathland over to Whitby

A dry, clear day with the warm autumn colours of the landscape reflected in the sky. It is only the additional blue that reminds you that nature is being deceptive; creating a memory of a mild autumn day when in fact it was a crisp cold day, one that takes your breath away. So cold was it that my only company whilst sketching were the two solitary birds. With this vast expanse of moorland in front of me, I could envisage what it must be like to view the world from above like those birds, as I stood on the moor with my feet firmly on the ground.

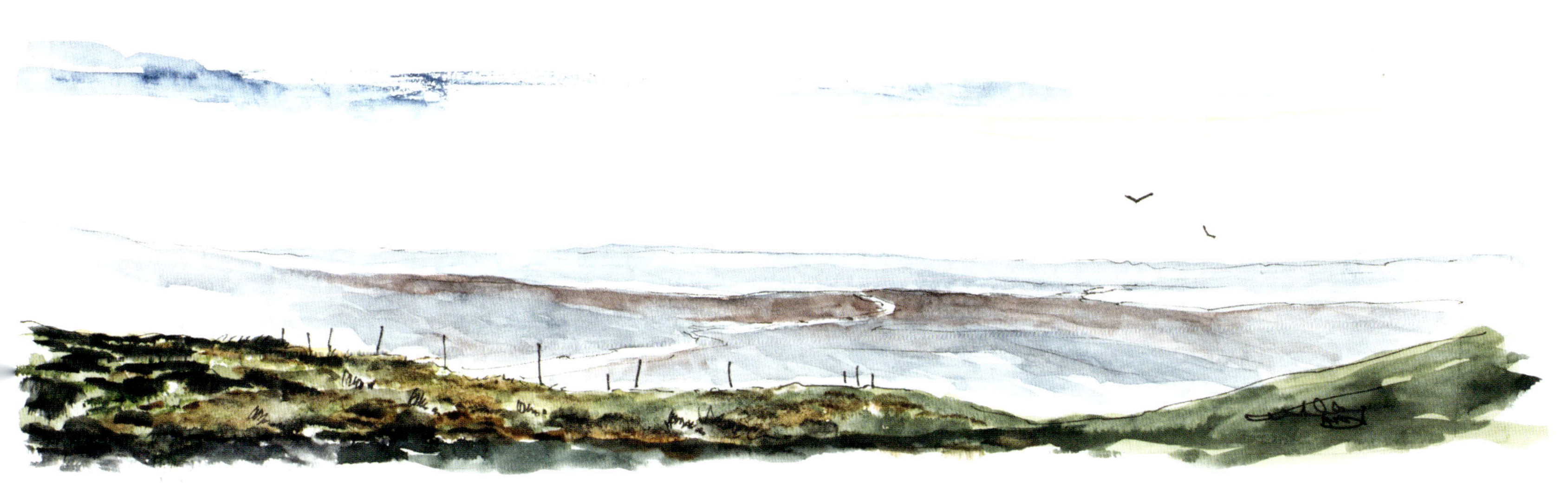

Goathland over to Whitby.

The Bridge, Langsett

Brookhouse Bridge crosses the Little Don, or Porter River, just before it enters the reservoir. In the summer I would recommend taking a detour upstream of the bridge as there is a lovely spot for a picnic and for paddling in the water.

The forestry plantation which covers much of the south-west shore of the reservoir looks like an area of devastation at present, but is being managed to help protect native woodland birds. As they say, you cannot make an omelette without breaking a few eggs. With the support of the Forestry Commission and RSPB, Yorkshire Water have felled most of the coniferous trees, but saved and protected key native trees. Replanting is in process to develop a new upland oak wood, which will be a habitat for woodland birds.

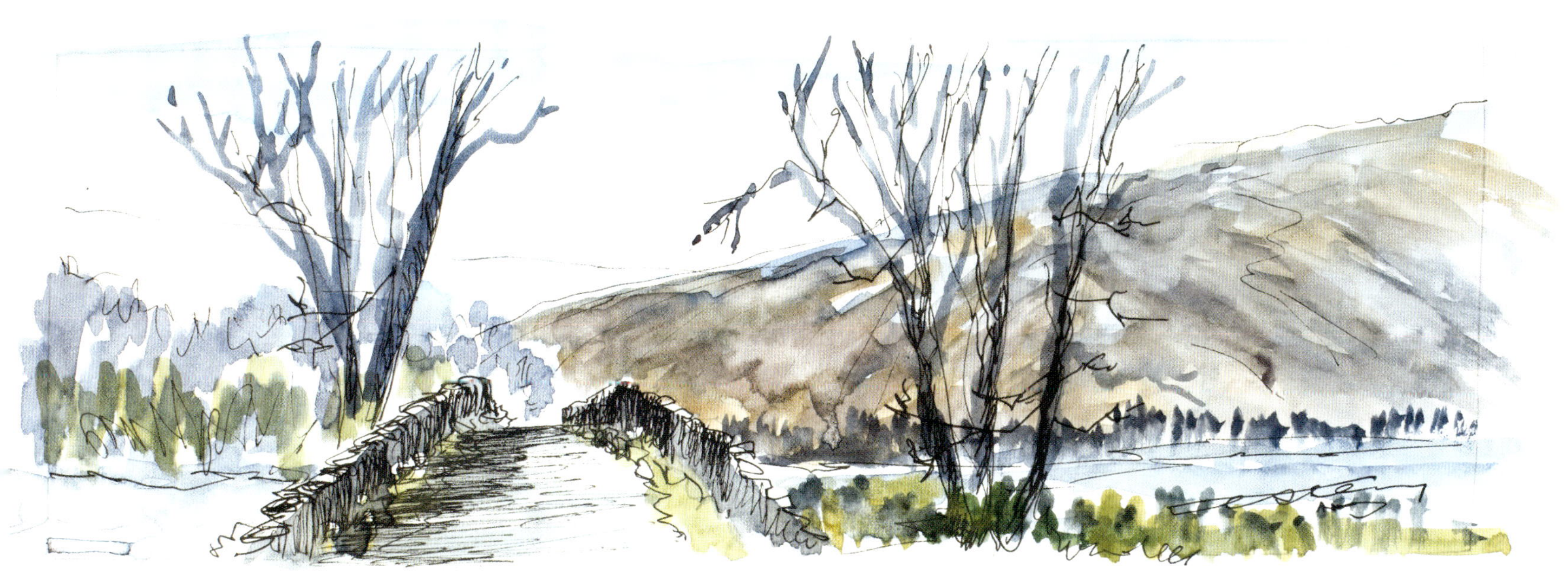

The Bridge, Langsett 37

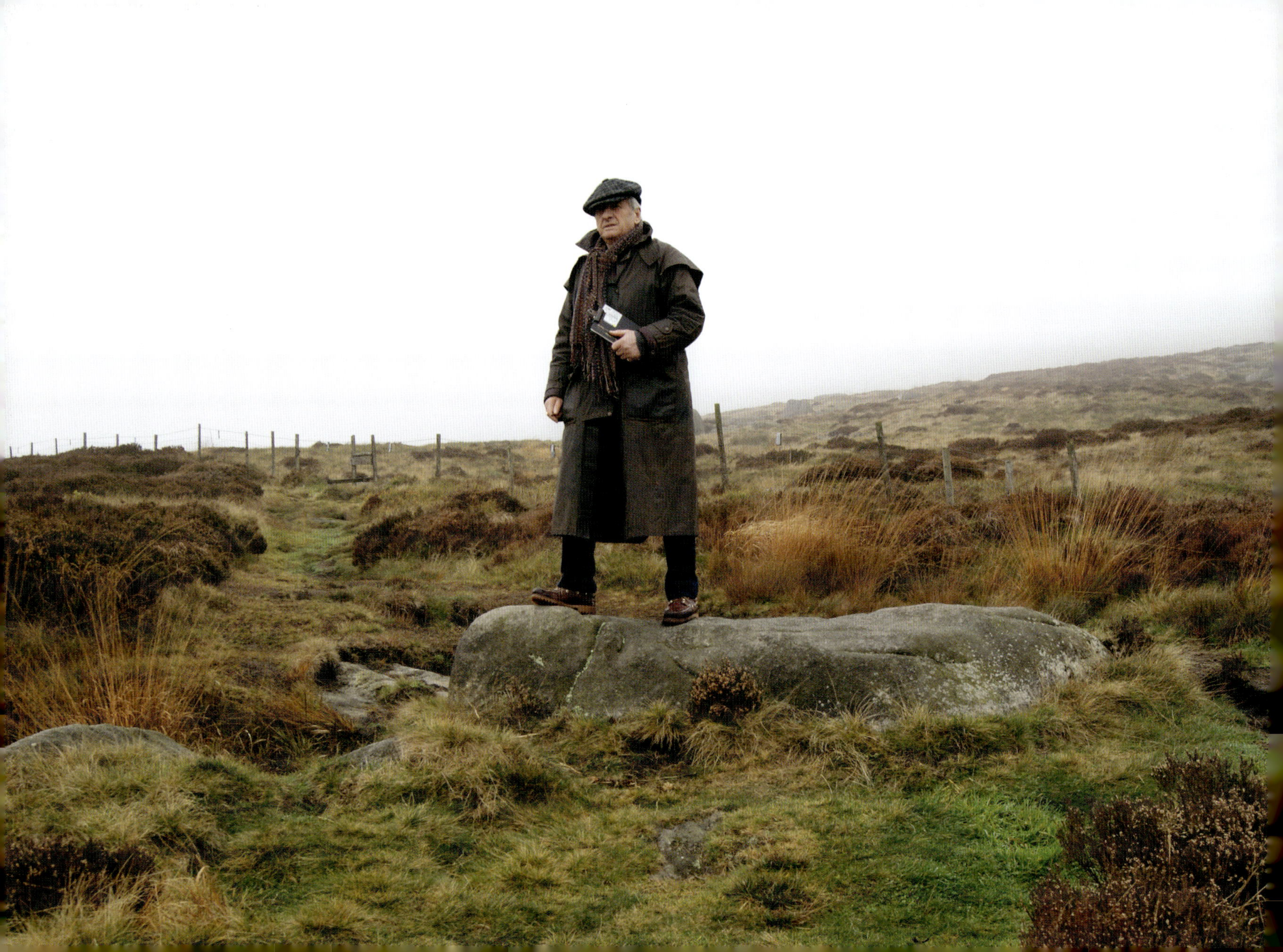

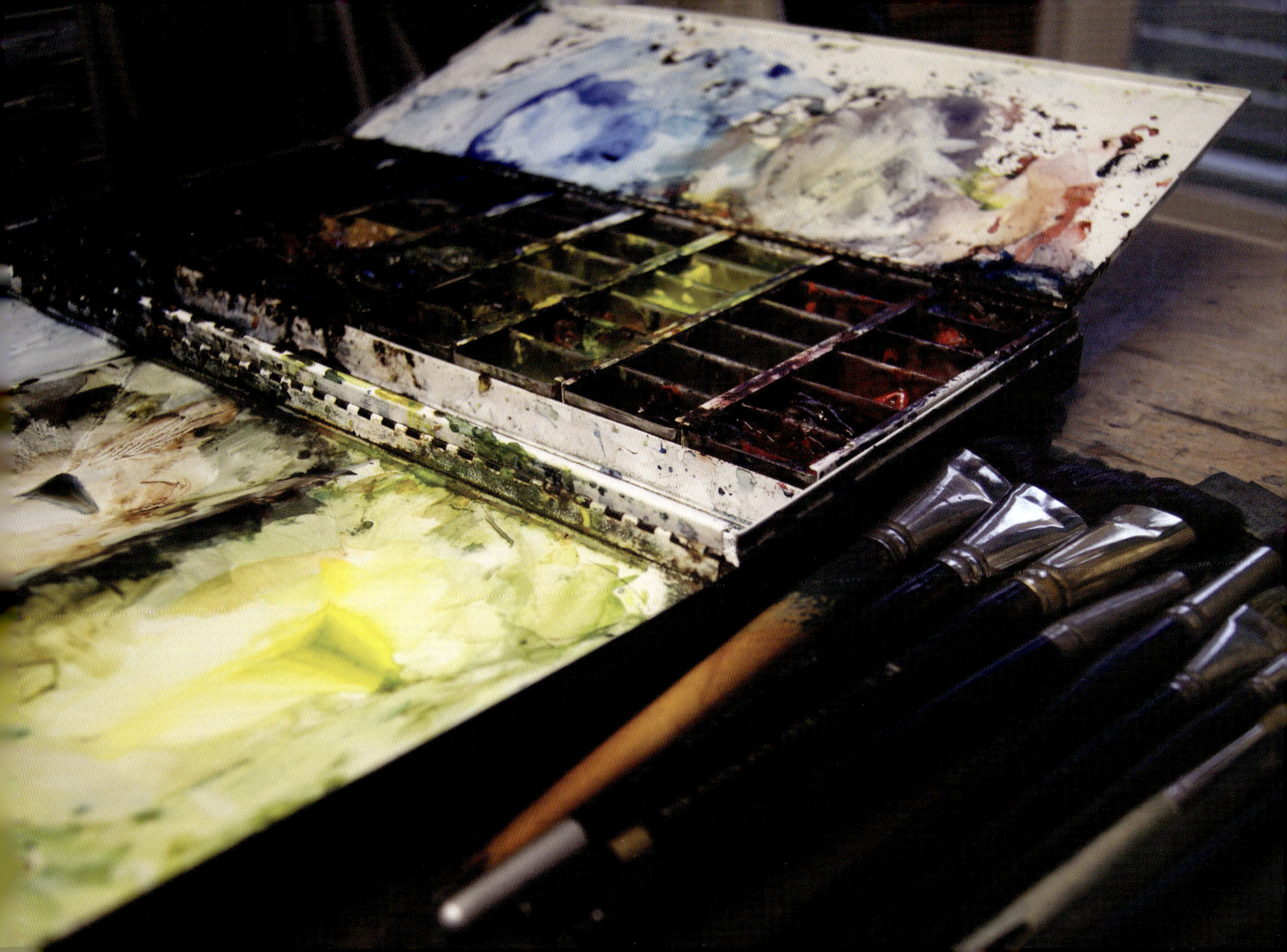

Heather Moorland, Langsett

The luminosity of the vivid green bilberry bushes, infiltrated with warm purple heather and rushes, up against the misty blue of the middle distance created a feast for the senses. I was fortunate, for it had rained in the days leading up to my venture, but Mother Nature was on my side and although overcast as I commenced the walk, there was no rain and the cloud did eventually break to leave a warm day.

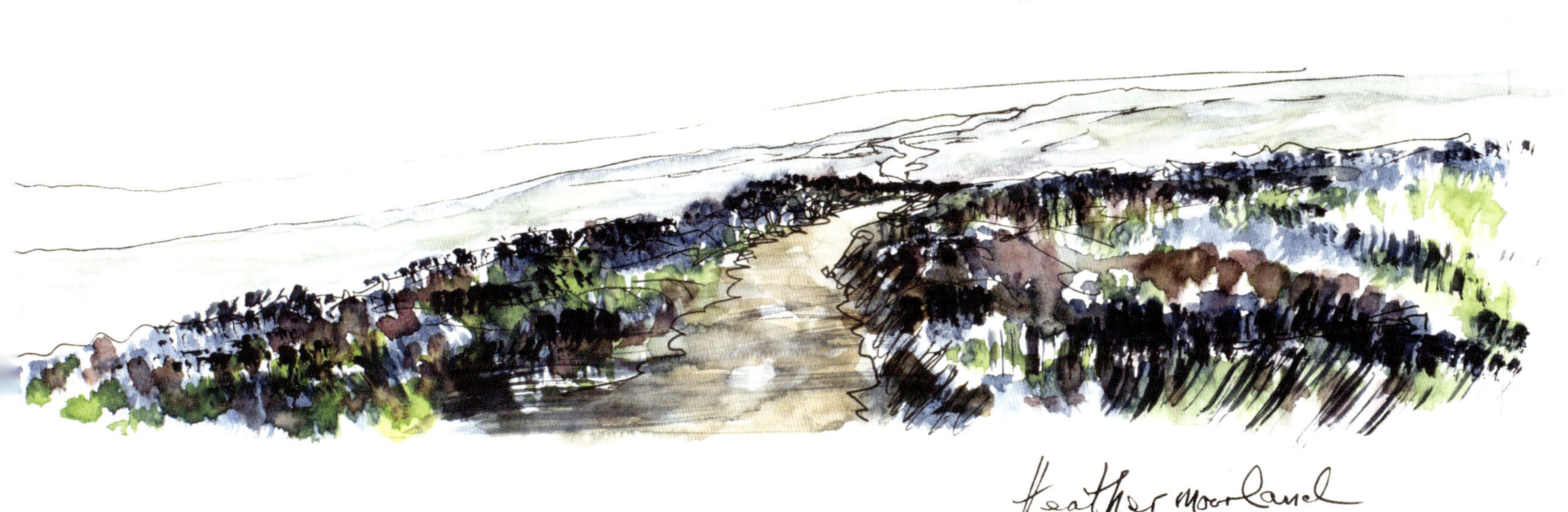

Heather Moorland, Langsett   41

North America, Langsett

Langsett Moor is one of my favourite walks through woodland and up on to open moorland. The paths channelled out between the heather and the bilberries spread out before you like dividing lines for a map of the earth. Parking in the Yorkshire Water car park, the footpath takes you along the reservoir edge before turning and beginning to climb out onto the exposed landscape, with a view that takes in the whole panorama. There is time for Yorkshire humour along the way as you pass the remaining stones of an old farm house, known as North America, so there is the ability to leave the country and return all in the space of a walk.

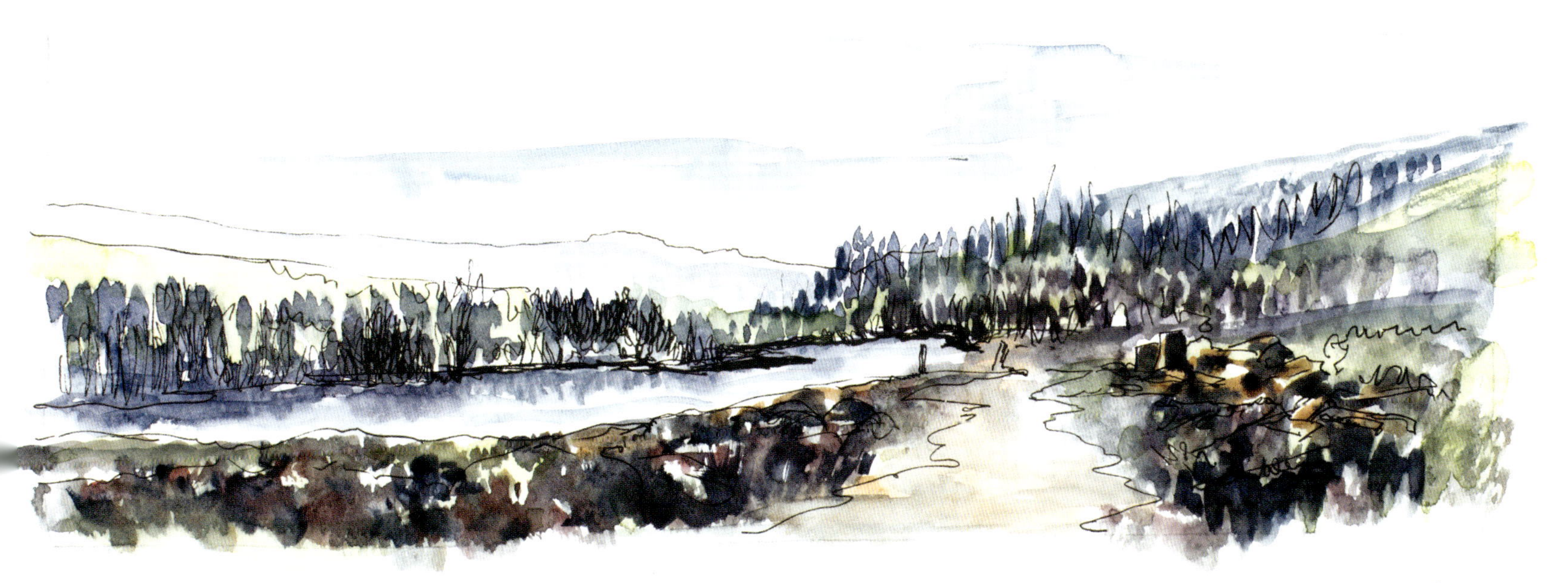

N. A. Farm Langsett Moor

Wind and Rain - Pack Horse Inn, near Widdop Moor

Pretty much in the middle of nowhere, you can imagine that this inn has sheltered many a weary traveller, as it stands solid as a sanctuary against the elements. Although I believe it is still used as an inn today, I have no experience of its hospitality. I enjoy venturing out on what are often the least hospitable days in order to capture the atmosphere, and can return home to realise I have not stopped to eat or drink all day, such is the excitement to transfer the drama to paper.

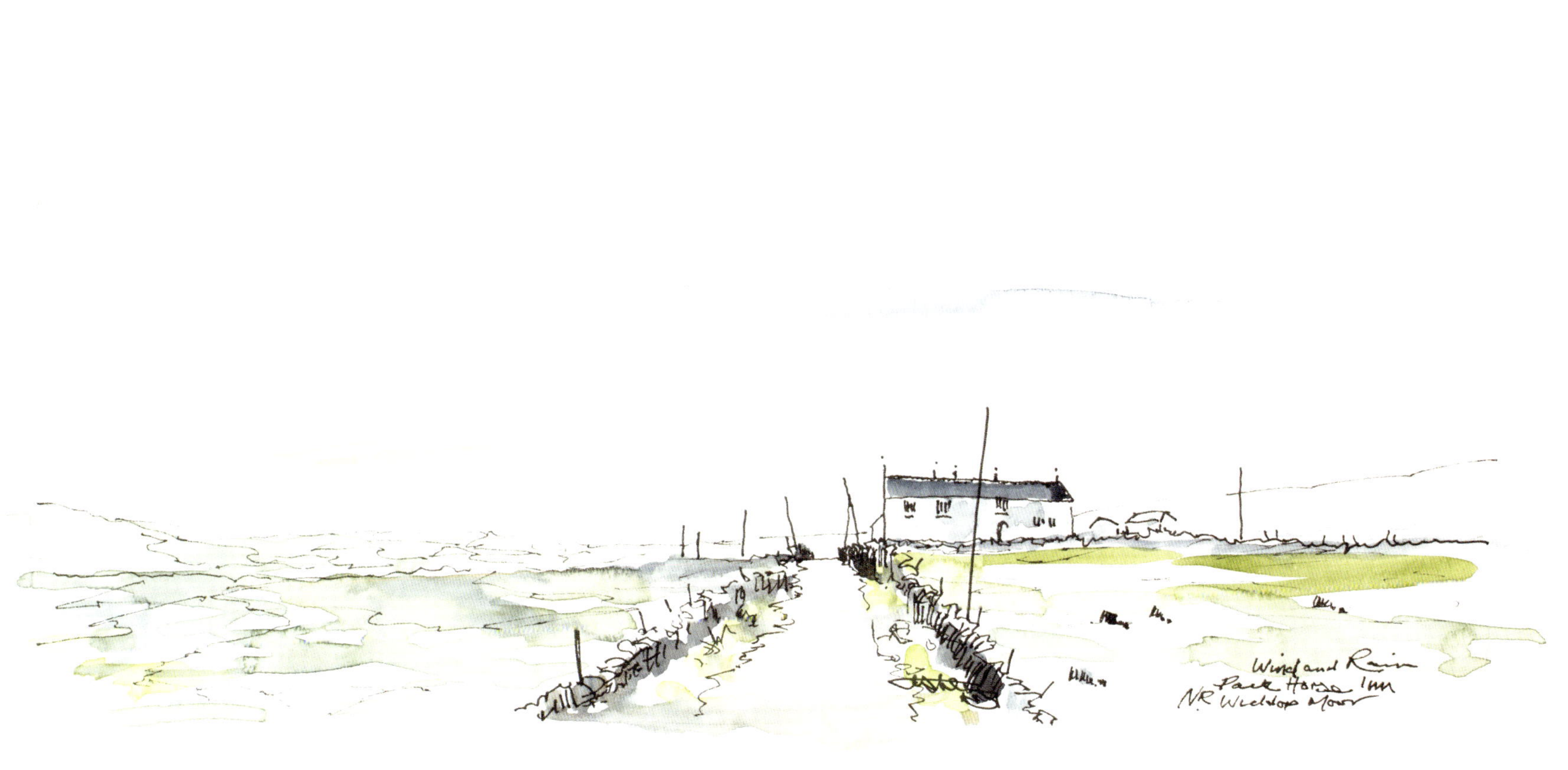

Wind and Rain
Pack Horse Inn
NR Widdop Moor

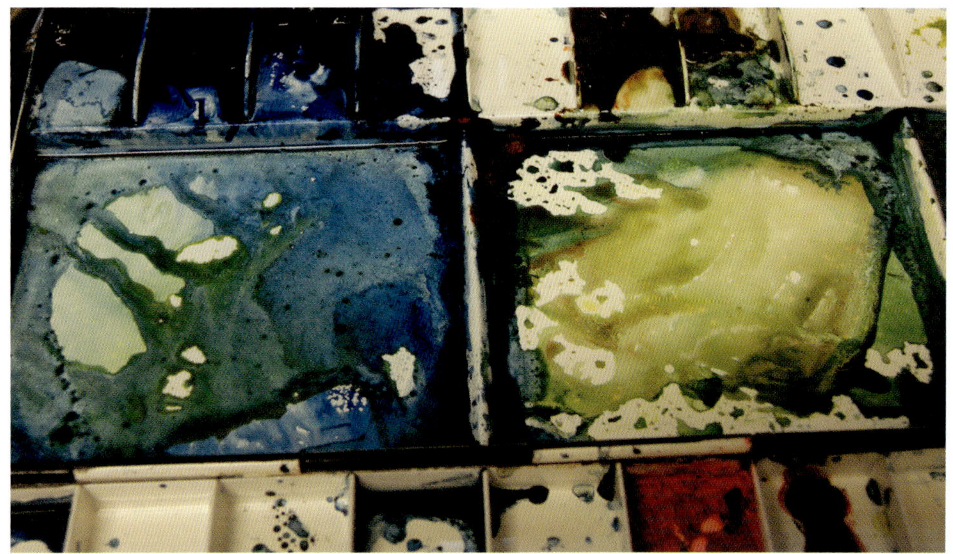

Staithes

I think the words of Edward Hopper articulates it so well, "If I could say it in words, there would be no reason to paint it". Sometimes no words are required, or at least I hope that is what people find when viewing my paintings. They are not just watercolours; they are a part of me and a three–way conversation between the artist, the landscape and then the viewer.

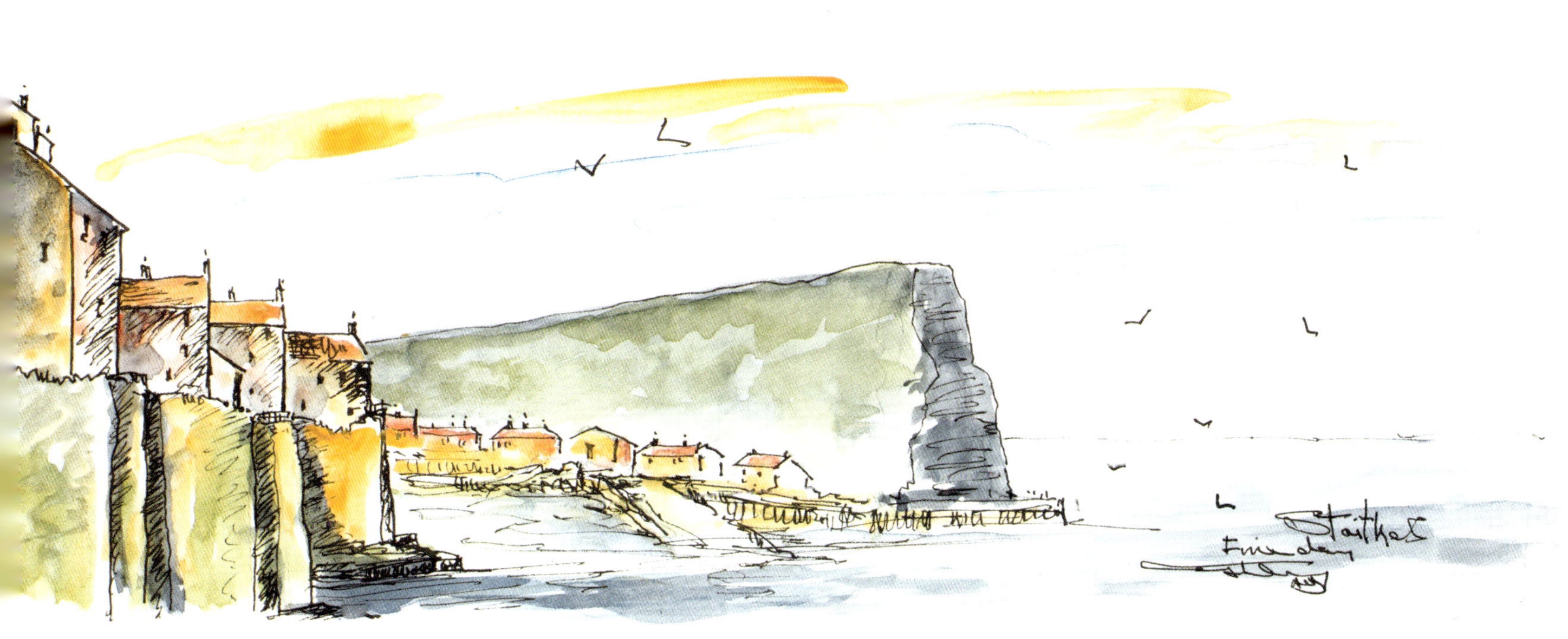

Heptonstall

Heptonstall is a hidden gem and a must for anyone who makes it to Hebden Bridge. Take a detour and park on the outskirts of this intricate village. Apart from Haworth, I have not visited another location like it. The Methodist Church, for which the foundation stone was laid by John Wesley himself, is an unusual octagonal build, "so that the devil could not hide in the corners". The grave of Sylvia Plath, the American poet who was married to Poet Laureate Ted Hughes, is situated in St Thomas a' Becketts church yard and the village was most recently shown on the television drama 'Happy Valley'. Prepare to spend a little time enjoying the landscape and then head to the café for a warming bacon sandwich and cup of tea.

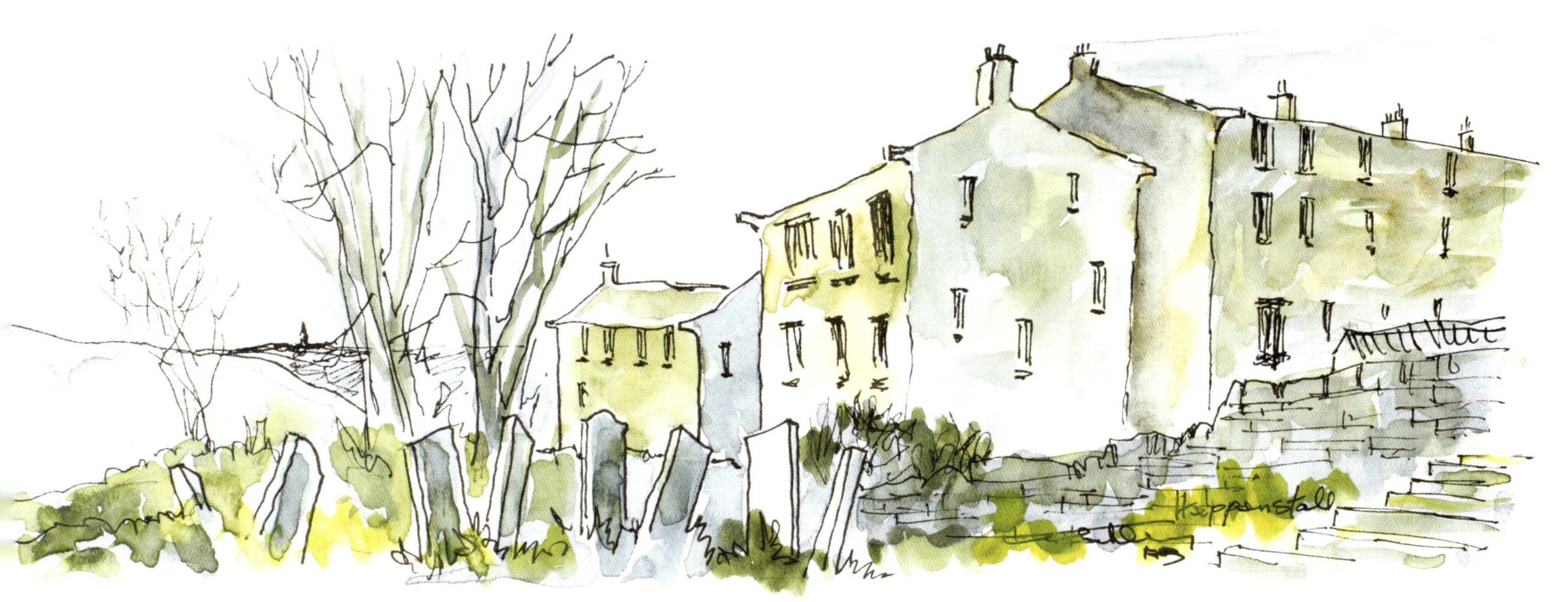

Dodd Fell

As they say, "All roads lead to Rome" and this one truly did. Created by the Romans it disappears into the distance, cutting a channel across the open moorland. It makes you think of the history of marching feet that have perhaps stood for a moment and taken in the very same view, one that I can only hope remains unchanged, but to do this we need to engage the next generation of guardians.

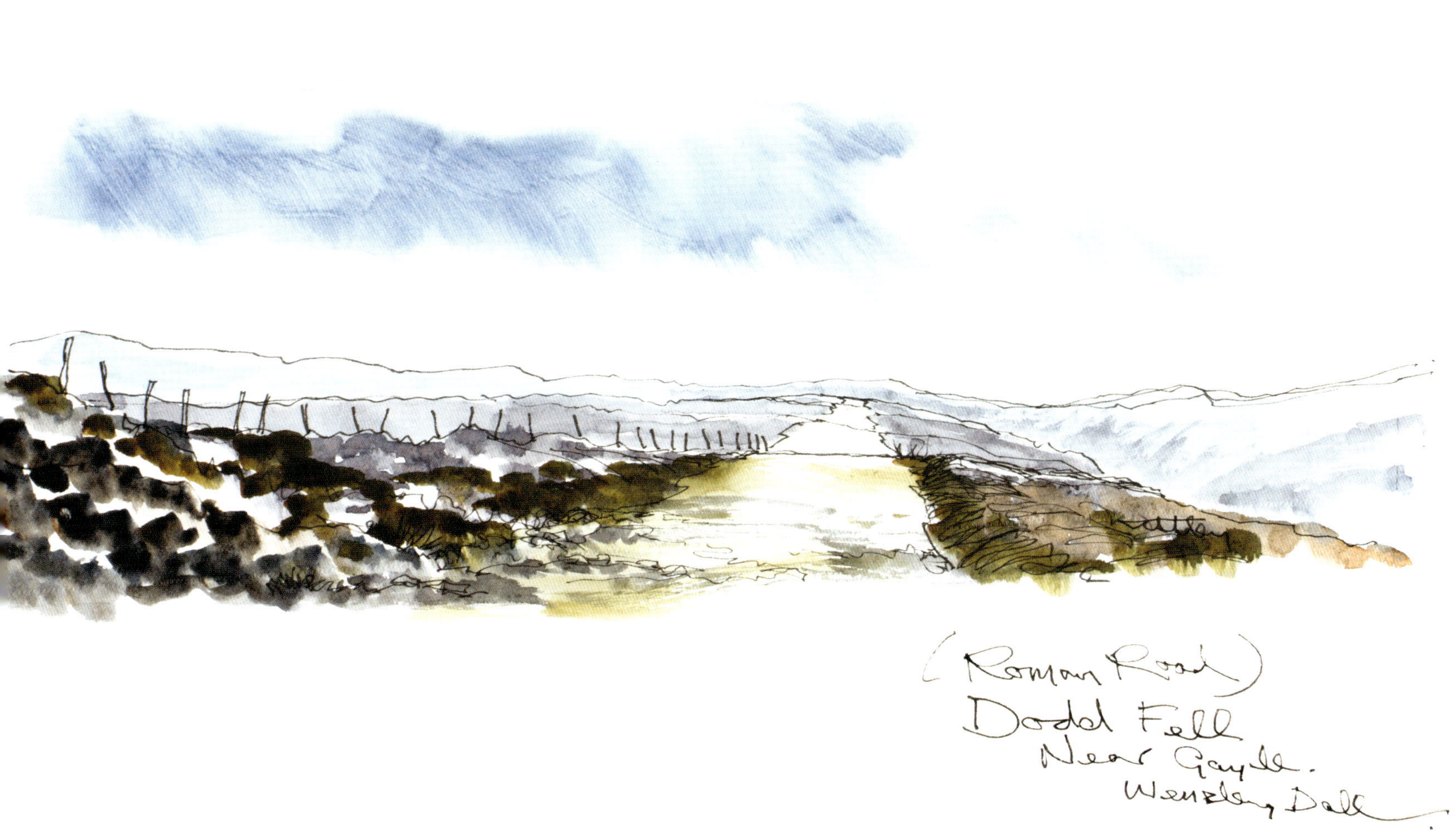

(Roman Road)
Dodd Fell
Near Gayle.
Wensley Dale

Wether Fell and Penyghent

As I stand on the open moorland, a hymn vividly comes to mind: 'Guide me oh thy great Redeemer'. I feel I have been guided, perhaps a stronger word would be compelled, to capture the landscape of Yorkshire and the Dales for over fifty years. A cine film taken of me at the age of twenty-five by John Hoyland, which was recently archived by the University of Huddersfield, seeks to explain this compulsion I had even then.

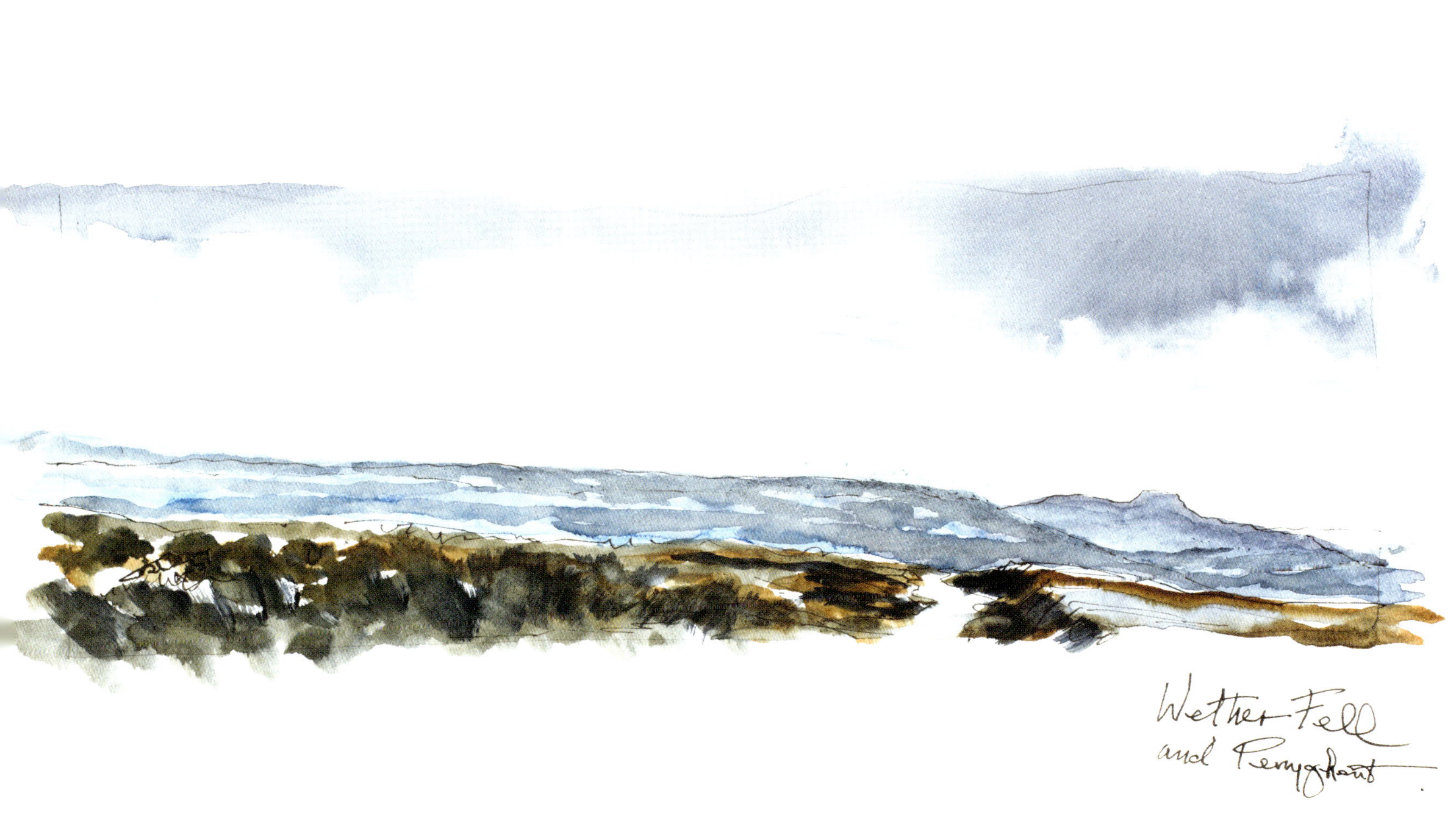

Wether Fell
and Penyghent

Scarborough Lighthouse

Originally built in 1809, the lighthouse has survived its own battles over the years, having been destroyed by a German Shell in the First World War and then rebuilt in 1939. Although the building is now home to the Scarborough Yacht Club, due to the sad decline of the fishing industry, the lighthouse is now only manned through the summer, but still remains a beacon of hope against the rock face.

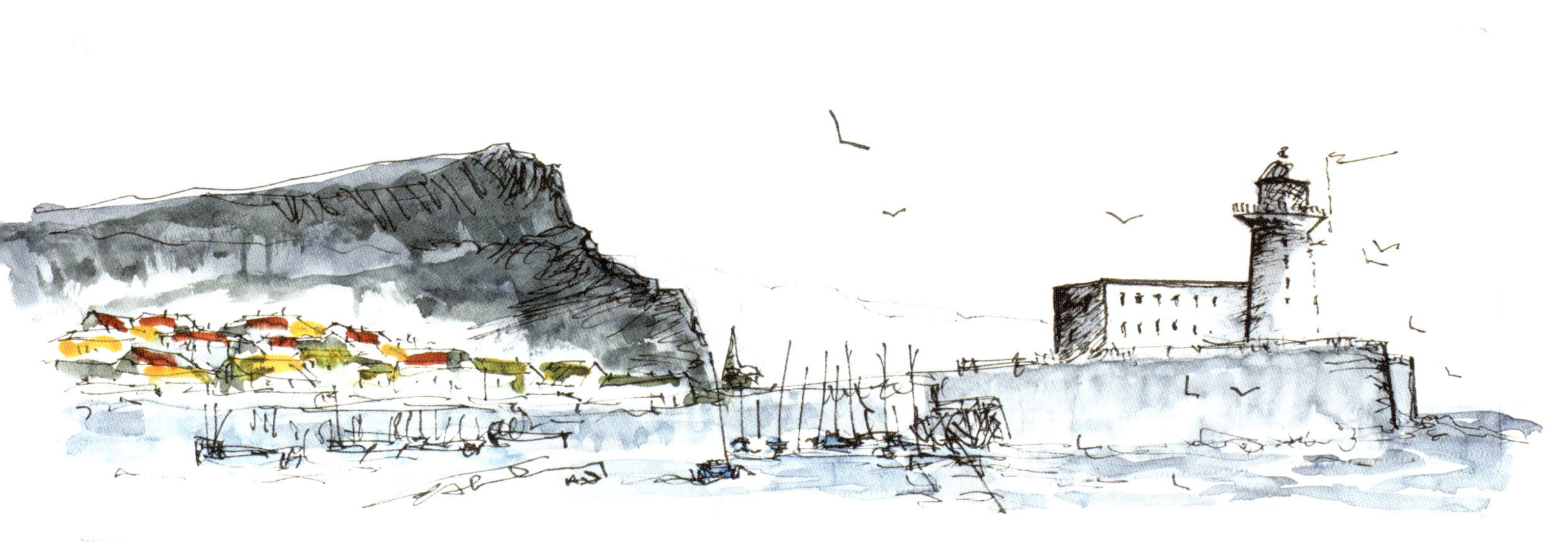

Scarborough Lighthouse

Black Sheep Inn, Wensleydale

It is always a question I ask myself: 'Do you choose the landscape or does it choose you?' Are those that work the land tending sheep or labouring the earth in inhospitable locations pulled by something more than an occupation? After all, even when weather conditions worsen they don't walk away. In fact, they walk into it head on because the farm is an extension of family. I know that I am where I need to be; close to the landscapes that fill my head and heart. It is a function that is as intrinsic to my being as the oxygen I require to breath.

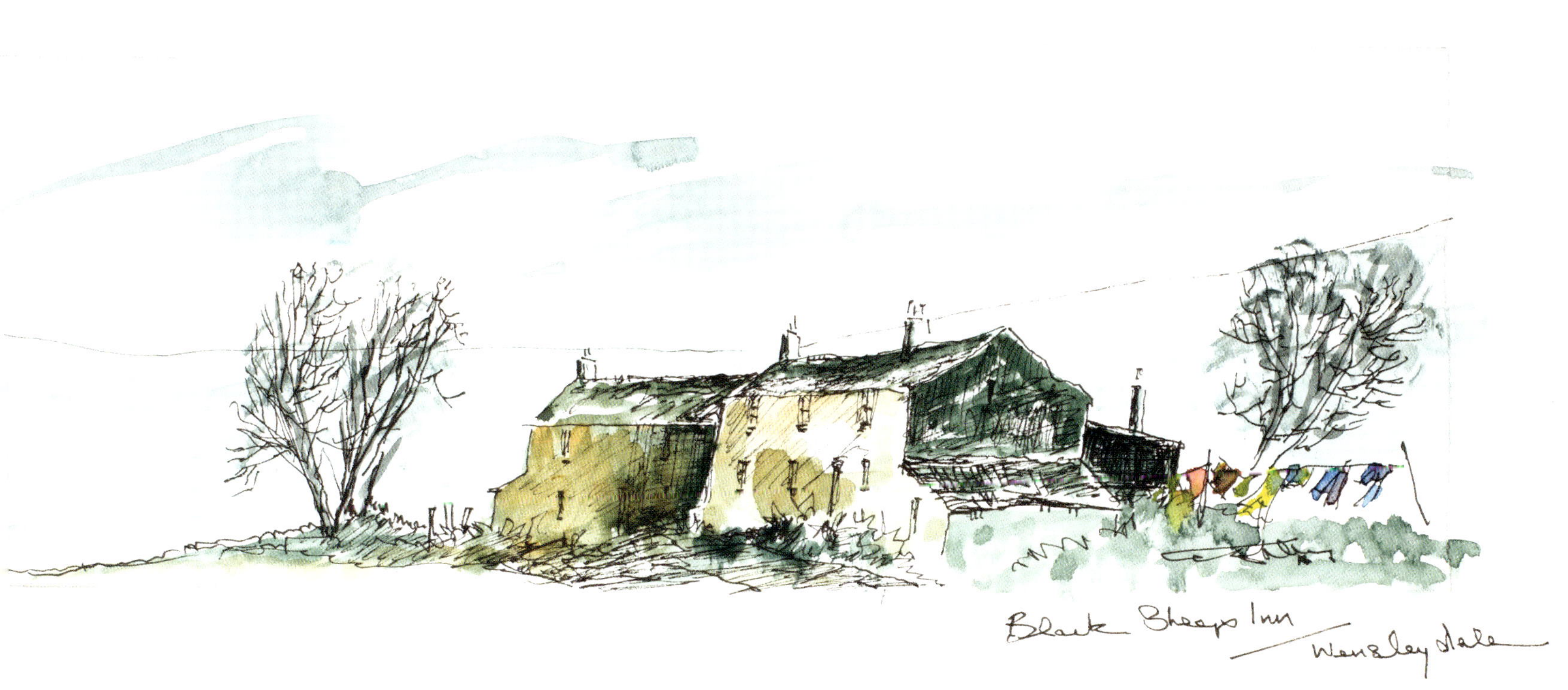
Black Sheep Inn
Wensley Dale

Roseberry Topping

A lesser taken viewing point of Roseberry Topping, hidden within Newton Moor Wood. Thanks to the National Trust, is now a location for a frame within the 'Framing the Landscape' project. Hidden within the trees amongst the ferns, the free standing frame is naturally camouflaged to blend in with the landscape and as you pass along the bottom edge of the wood, why not stop for a minute and admire the view.

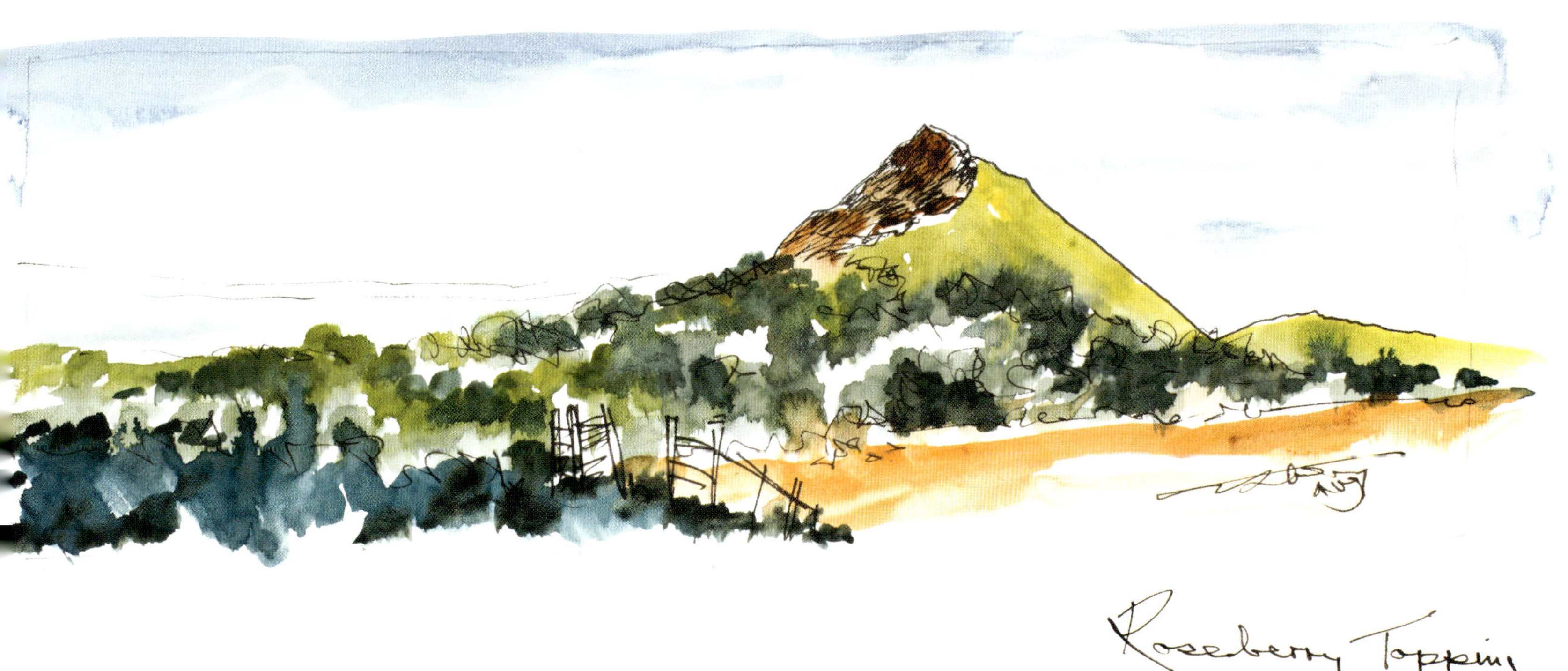

Roseberry Topping

From Grassington to Burnsall

A little unusual for me I know; a tranquil meadow at the side of the Grassington to Burnsall Road. Over the wall, the sheep are minding their own business, whilst the sun hitting the grassy meadow creates a contrast with the blue receding hills. It seems that all is well with the world and God's Own County – Yorkshire. I often think to myself how it would stir my soul if I could unfold my arms, hands out to the breeze and sweep across the landscape like a bird gaining a new perspective, not only looking forward, but down on the wide expanse. It must be exhilarating.

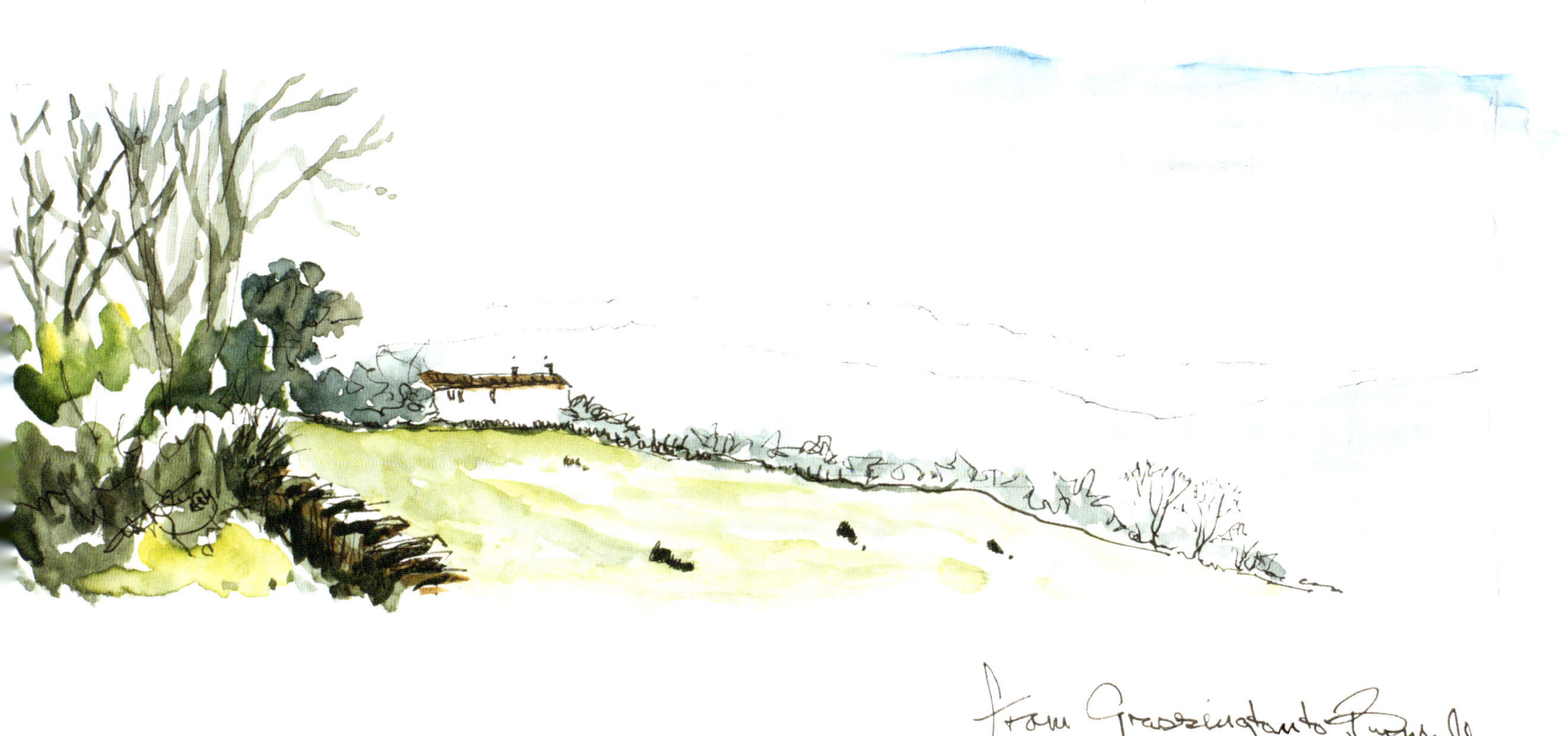

From Grassington to Burnsall
'GRASS MEADOWS'

Old Barns

Scattered across the Moors and Dales like relics to a bygone era, the barns stand firm; a sanctuary from the prevailing winds made evident by the leaning posts. There is so much to read from the landscape if we just take the time to look. As I get older, my need to absorb and make memories of these landscapes is like a insatiable thirst. There is so much we miss when we believe we have time on our side. As we grow older, these are the simple things we relish, should it all be taken from us in the blink of an eye.

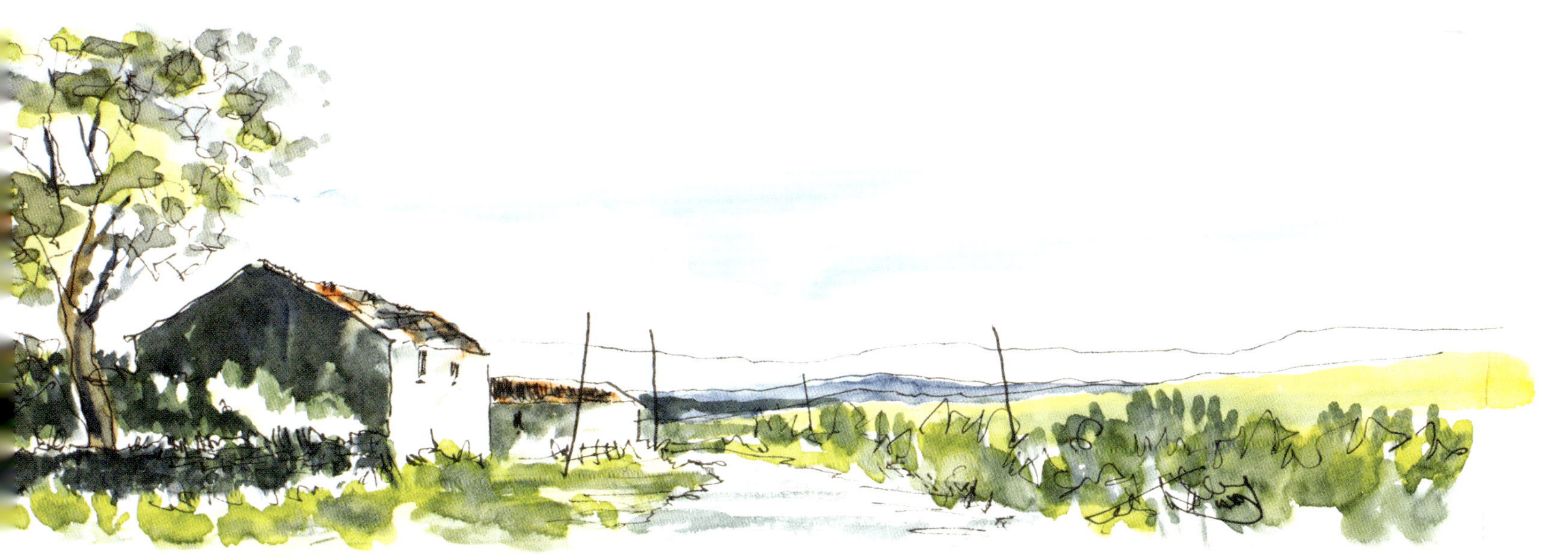

'Old Barns'
Looking to Grassington

Bridleway on Road Side from Grassington to Burnsall

The open gateway appears to beckon me on to the bridleway. With only 2.5 miles to Blea Beck it would be a pleasant walk to the water, particularly on this bright morning. I consider this sketch a tribute to the skills of the dry stone worker, for the walls will remain long after we are gone, as long as others leave them alone.

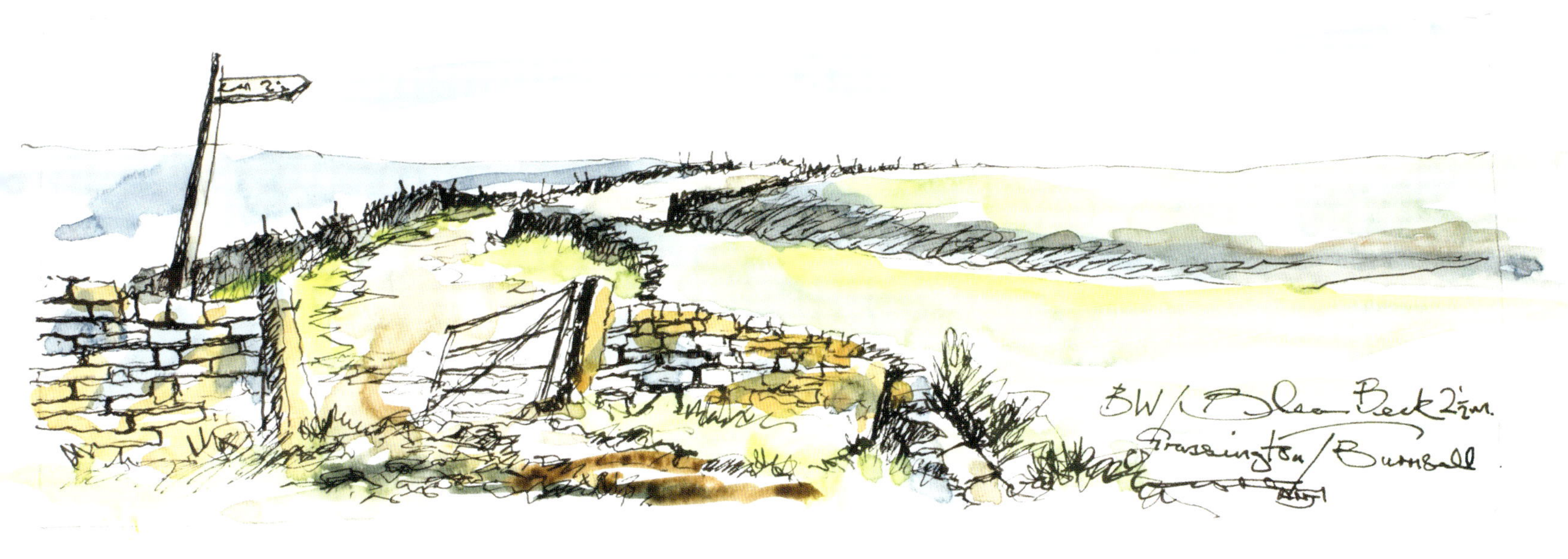
BW / Blea Beck 2½M.
Grassington / Burnsall.

Marsden Moor

Just up the road from my gallery in Holmfirth, Wessenden, Marsden Moor is a place of tranquillity; a moorland where I can reconnect with my mistress. It doesn't matter how long it has been since my last visit, it feels like she awaits to greet me with open arms, which ignites my passion for the Yorkshire landscape.

It is here on Marsden Moor that 'Framing the landscape' was launched with the very first frame. Nature has now blended the uncoated grey steel to muted earth tones, fitting of the landscape where it resides.

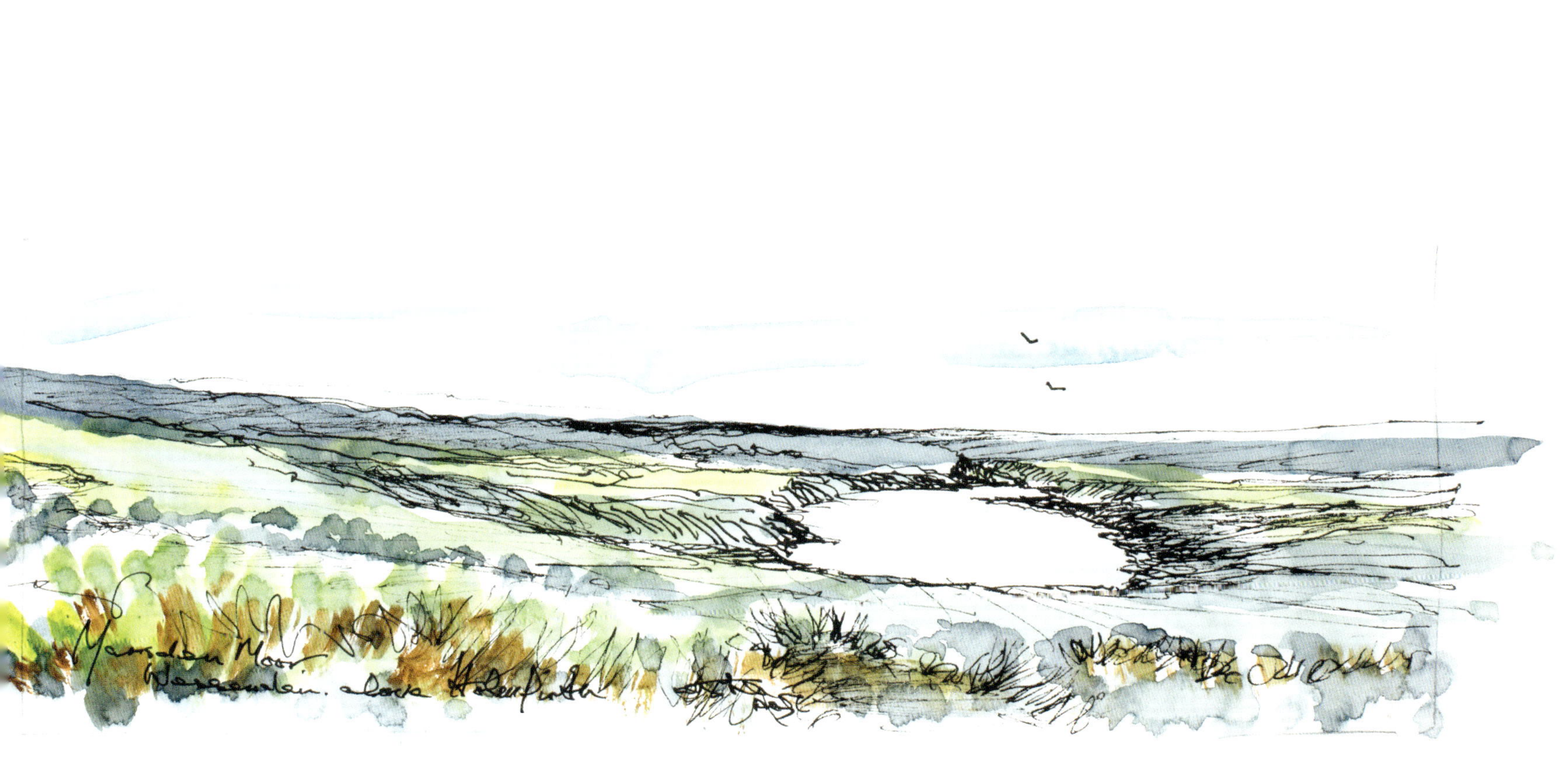

Runswick Bay

It is only the small boats that give an indication of the wind in what would otherwise look like a calm day. The dramatic crag of Lingrow Knowle provides a natural shelter for the red-roofed cottages and the sandy beach below it, showing a period in time when man worked in harmony with the landscape rather than against it. If you are planning a visit to Whitby, with only 9 miles separating the two, do make time for Runswick Bay; it is well worth the visit.

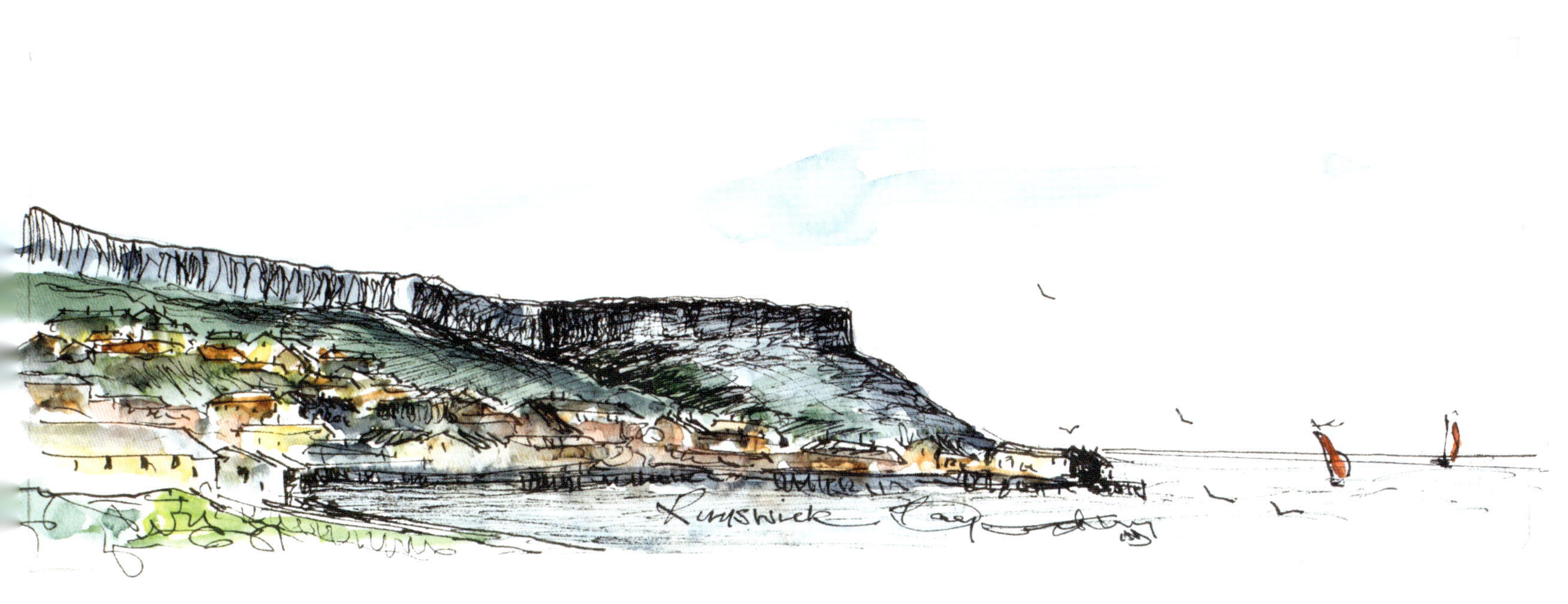

Appletreewick

What a fantastic name for a village in the Yorkshire Dales. Just its name alone conjures up an idyllic hamlet where the sun always shines. Most people who choose to venture for a day out mainly do so after hearing the weather reports for a dry day, not many would choose to go out knowing it was going to rain. As most of you who know my paintings will be aware, rain is not something that stops me sketching and this day was no exception.

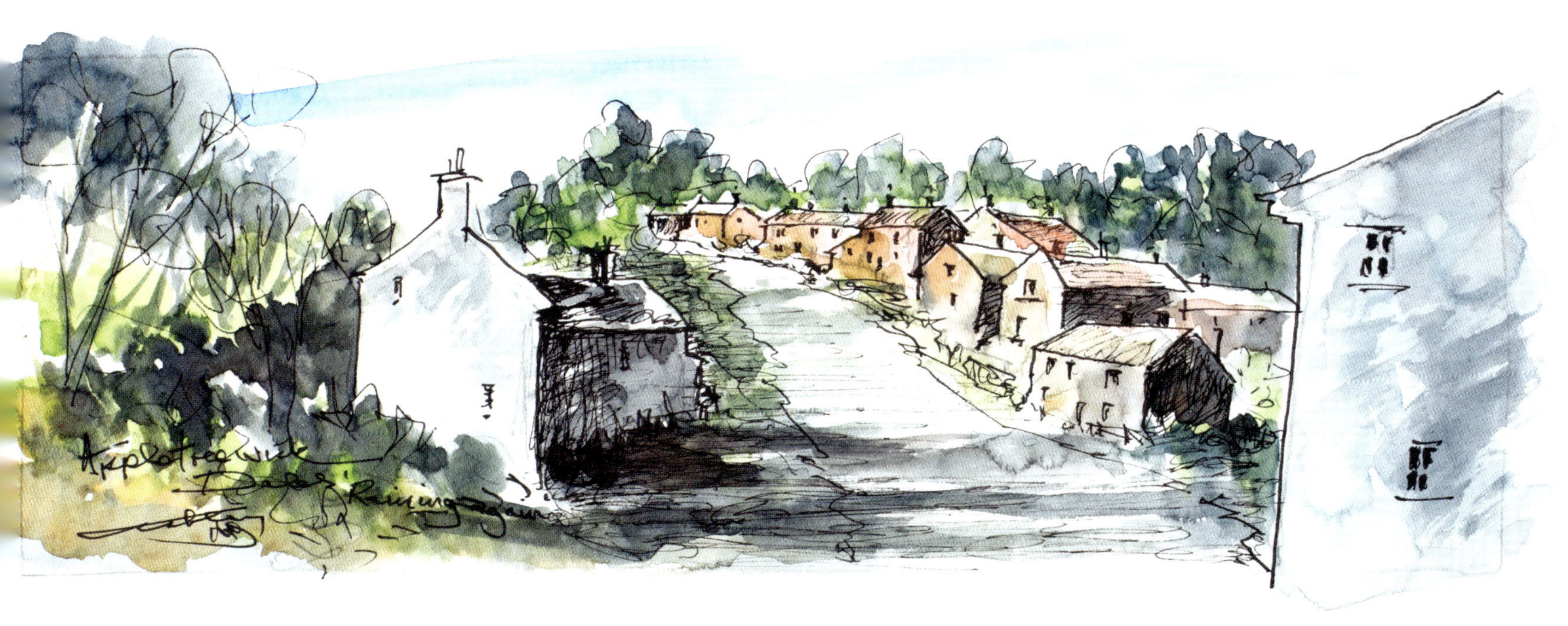

From Grassington to Ripley

Spring is on its way and the calmness of the farm belies the busy time of year it is for farmers. I think this must have been well on its way to lunch time, with the farmer and his family perhaps sitting down for a well-earned meal. It is a hard toil to make a living from the land and I have a great respect for those who do.

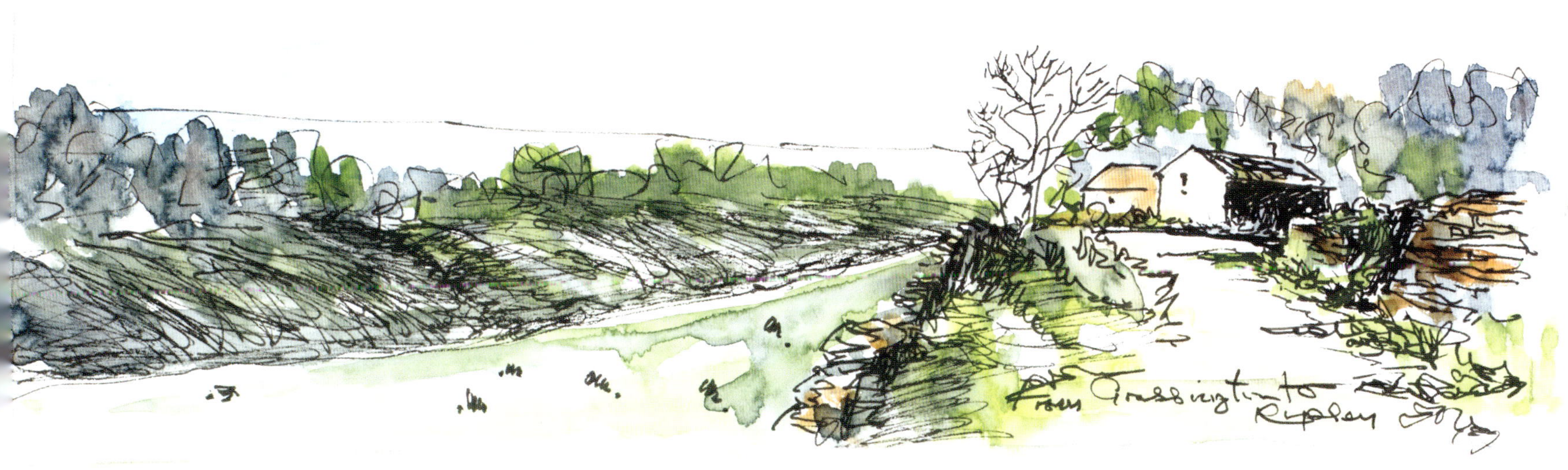

Farm, Hebden, Wharfedale

The end of the road is in sight for many a walker through Hebden. The village itself straddles a cross roads, with the road to the north taking you to the small hamlet of Hole Bottom; only in Yorkshire could you find such names and what a gift, making people smile as they repeat the names in their head.

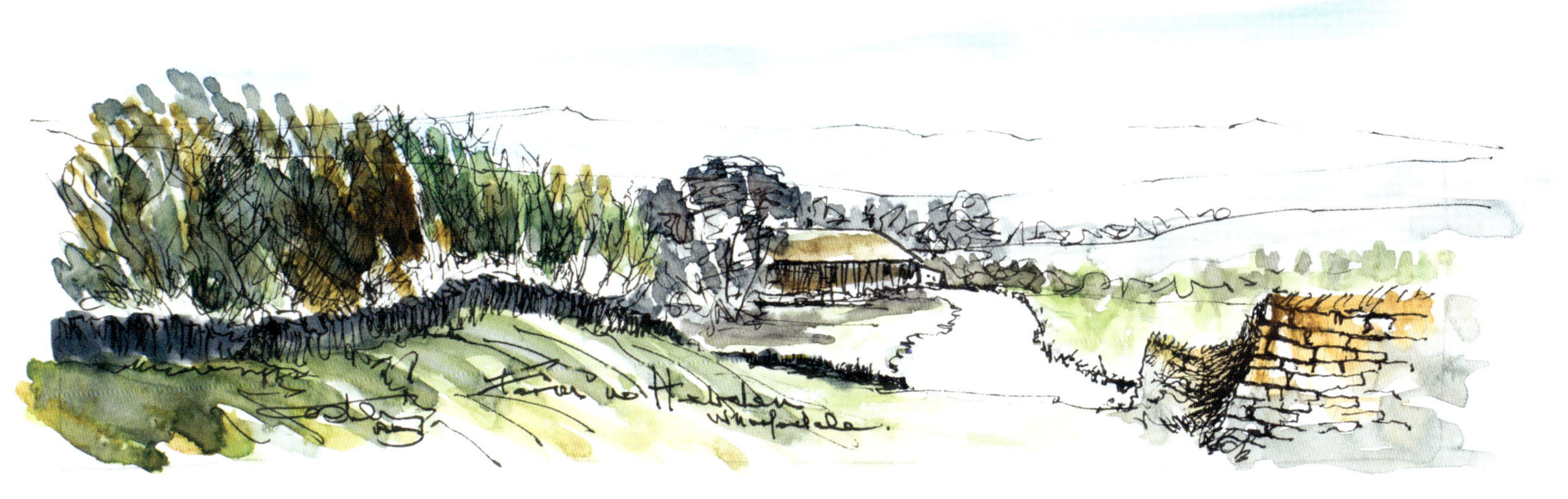

On the Roof of Yorkshire - Coming Down from Black Hill

This is above Holmfirth. What can I say? Where heaven and earth meet and the vista is a panorama allowing you to see for miles on a clear day. I know that those who enjoy walking and sketching will also get this 'wow' feeling, it starts with the eyes but reaches quickly down to your heart. I hope this feeling never dies, or that I go before it diminishes, for it would be a sad day to step onto the moors and see my mistress as if the relationship was over.

I am proud to have been able to frame this landscape in partnership with the University of Huddersfield and by permission of Yorkshire Water, so that from the car park at Holme Moss, a free standing aperture brings focus to the landscape.

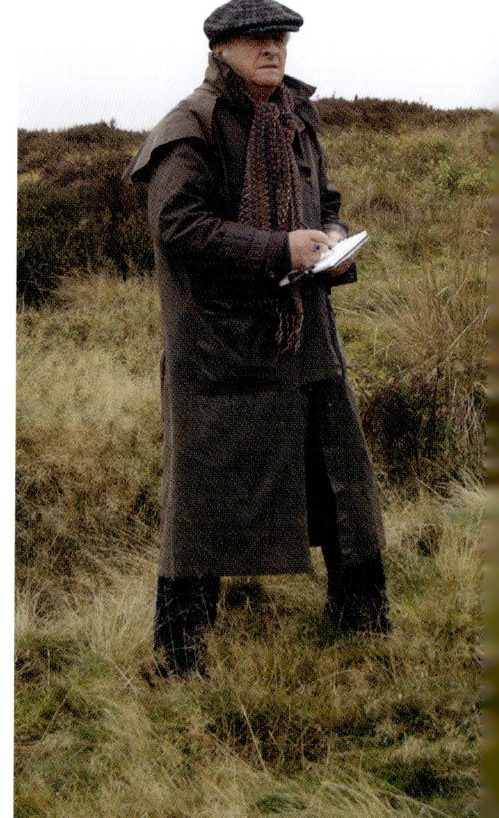

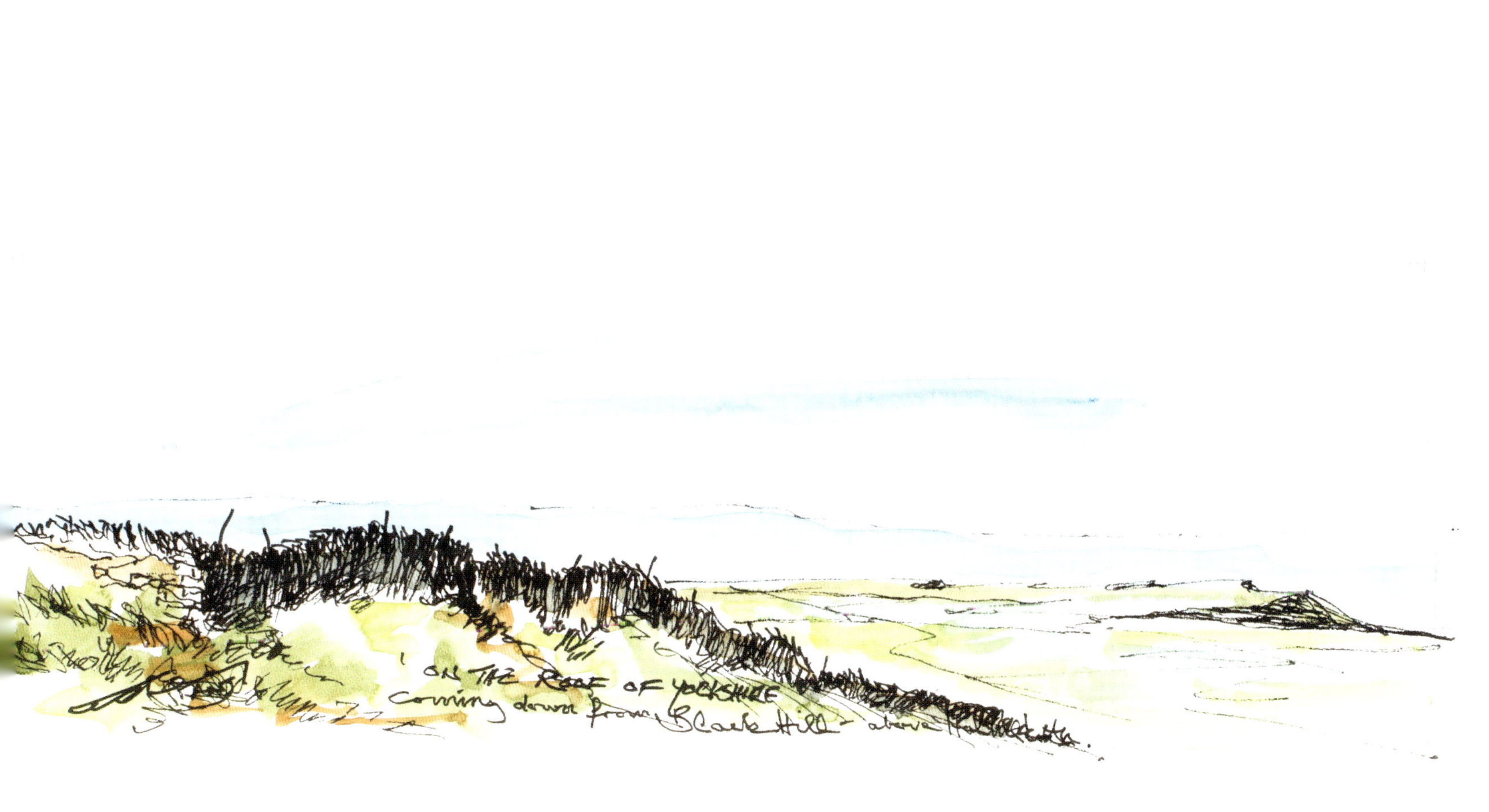
ON THE ROOF OF YORKSHIRE
Coming down from Black Hill - above Holmfirth.

River Ure, near Hawes

The River Ure is the principal river of Wensleydale, which is one of the only Yorkshire Dales to not be named after the river that runs through it, but after a village instead. It appears to meander through the valley as if it has all the time in the world. I too embraced this 'pause in time' to listen to the river as it flowed across the stones, the birds in flight and the sheep quiet as boulders in the field. We often need to take time out to appreciate the simple things around us.

Once the river reaches the falls at Aysgarth, much of its calmness depends on any previous rainfall, meaning it can range from a trickle to a torrent from day to day. This is Yorkshire and no two days or landscapes are the same.

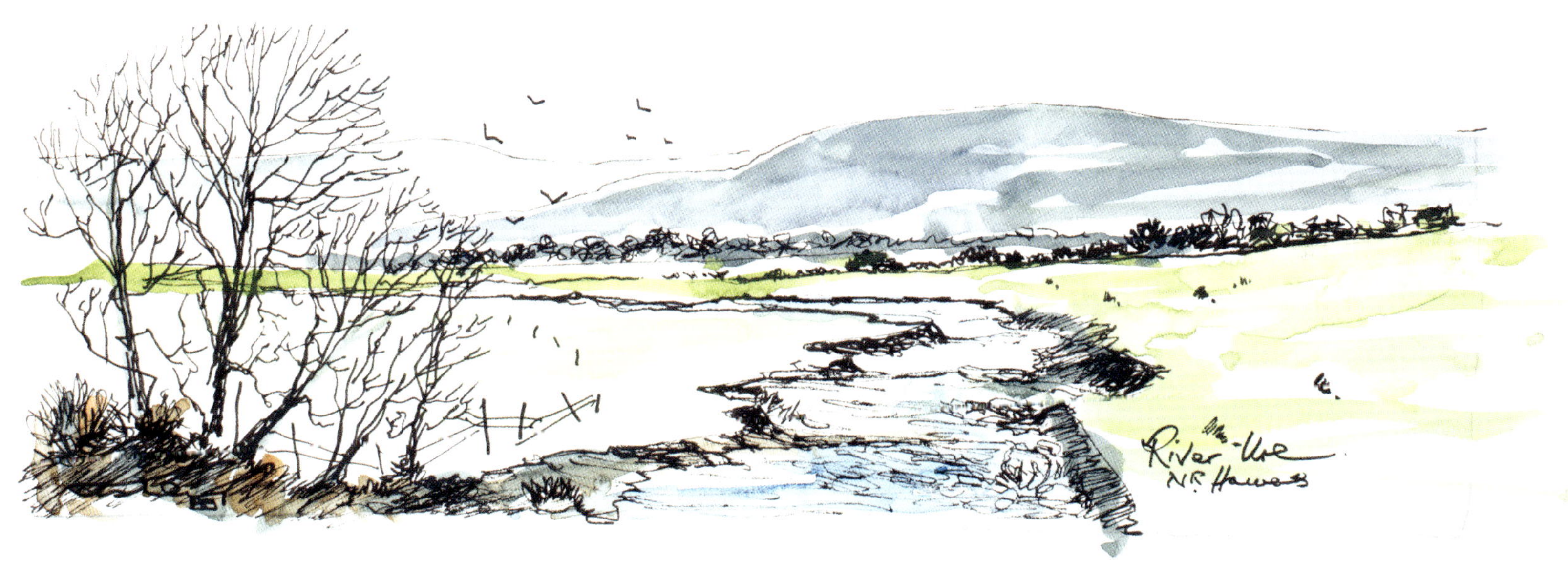

River Ure, near Hawes 79

Farm near Greenhow Hill and Stump Cross Cavern

It is hard to believe that often as much goes on underground as it does over ground, and the caverns are one such phenomenon. There is so much to see and do in Yorkshire; from coast to moorland, the landscape is at our very heart.

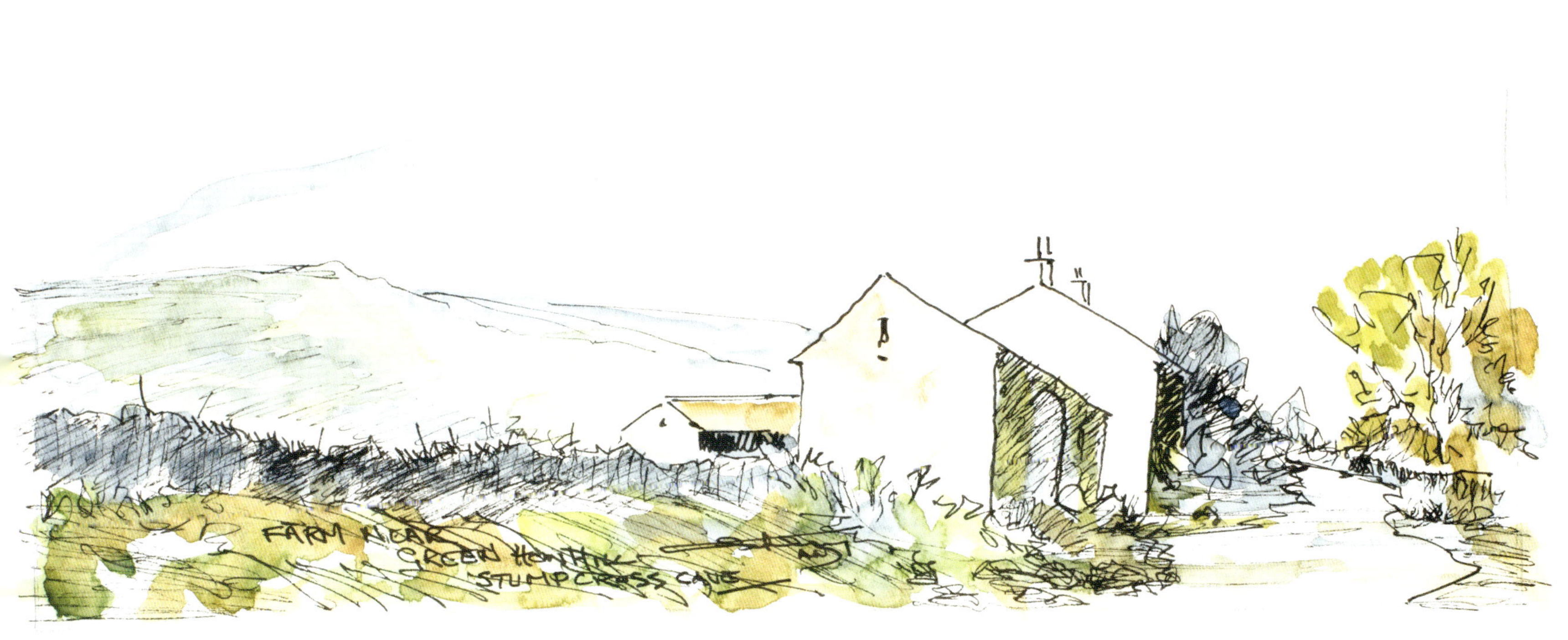

Farm near Greenhow Hill and Stump Cross Cavern   81

Near Hawes, Wensleydale

The name Hawes means 'a pass between mountains' and it stands between the stunning Buttertubs and Fleet Moss.

Hawes always brings to mind pleasant memories, for it was here that my wife and I would bring our young children for our holiday, staying at the caravan site and walking to the centre for replenishments of supplies. I see that the rope maker is still evident and that the Hawes Dairy, championed by Kit Calvert, is now the award winning and internationally renowned Wensleydale Creamery. Hawes is still very much a thriving market town, with Tuesday its official market day.

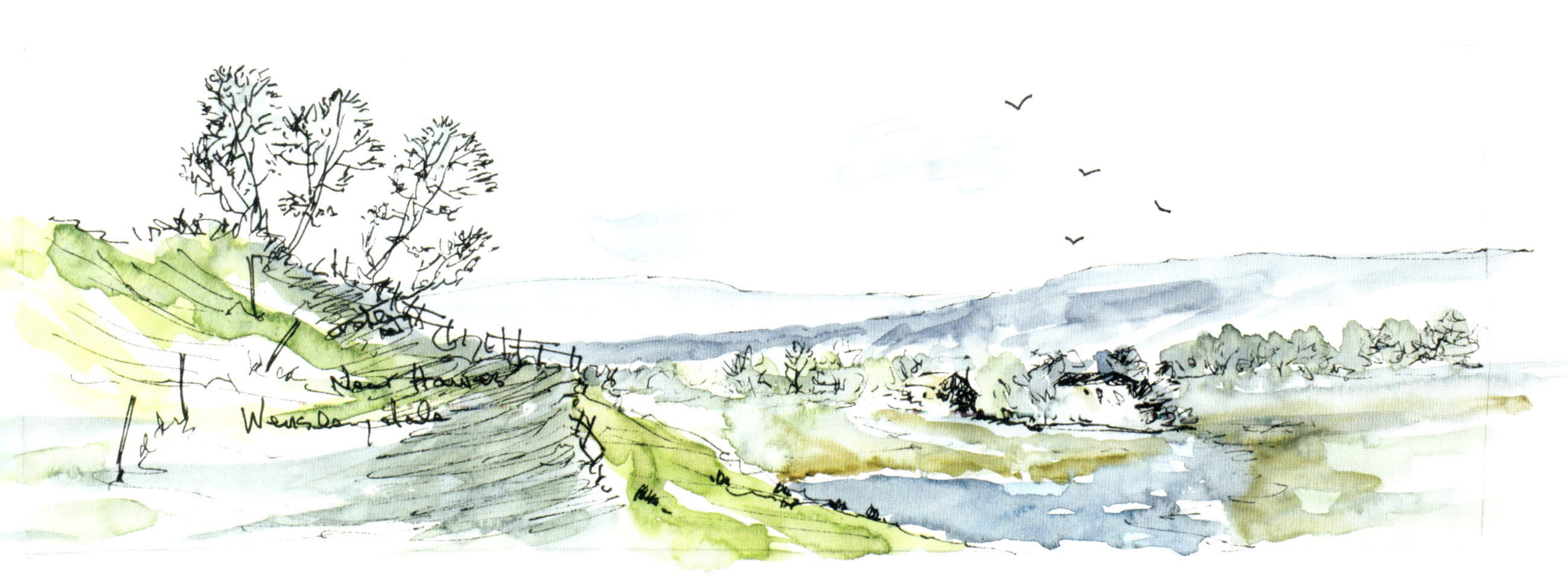

Near Hawses
Wensleydale

River Ure, near Aysgarth

This feels very much like the calm before the storm, as this gentle meandering river provides a false sense of security before the falls at Aysgarth. After heavy rains, the falls can be spectacular and dangerous at the same time.

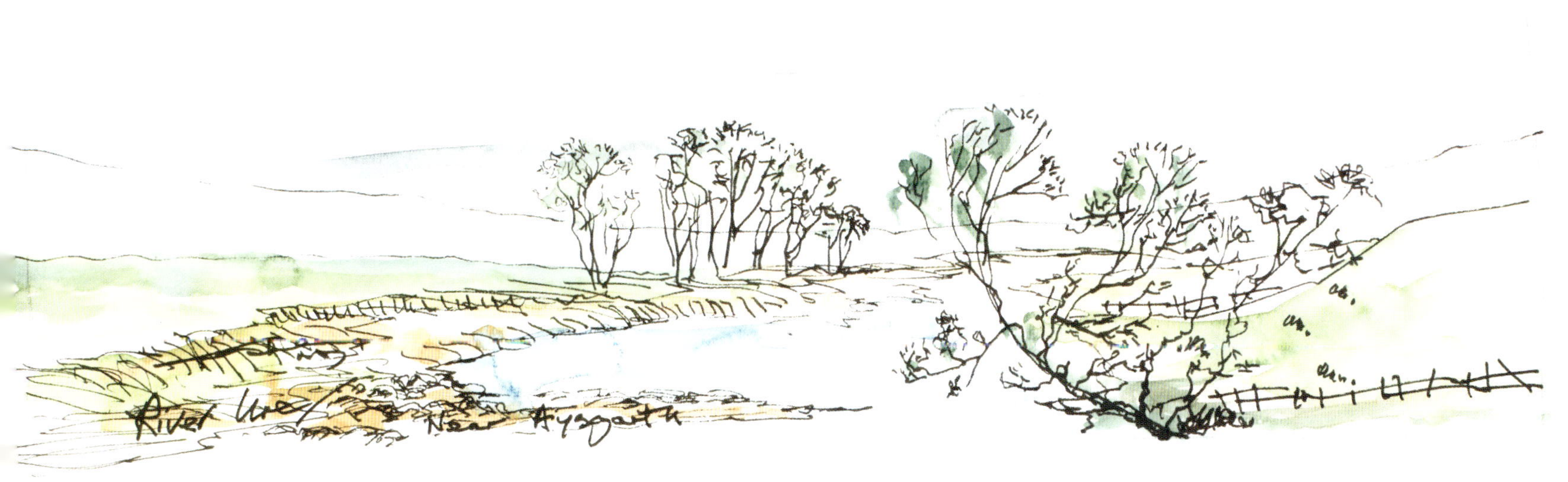

River Ure, near Aysgarth   85

The Green Dragon Inn, Hardraw Falls

The Green Dragon is a privately owned inn containing many of its original features; from the stone flags and timber beams to the roaring fires on a cold winter day. It also has a depth of history with JWM Turner having stayed here on one of his tours of Yorkshire. The inn is also the entrance to Hardraw Scaur Waterfall, or Hardraw Force, which is at its most fierce after heavy rainfall and its 100 feet drop is most impressive once reached through the ancient woodland.

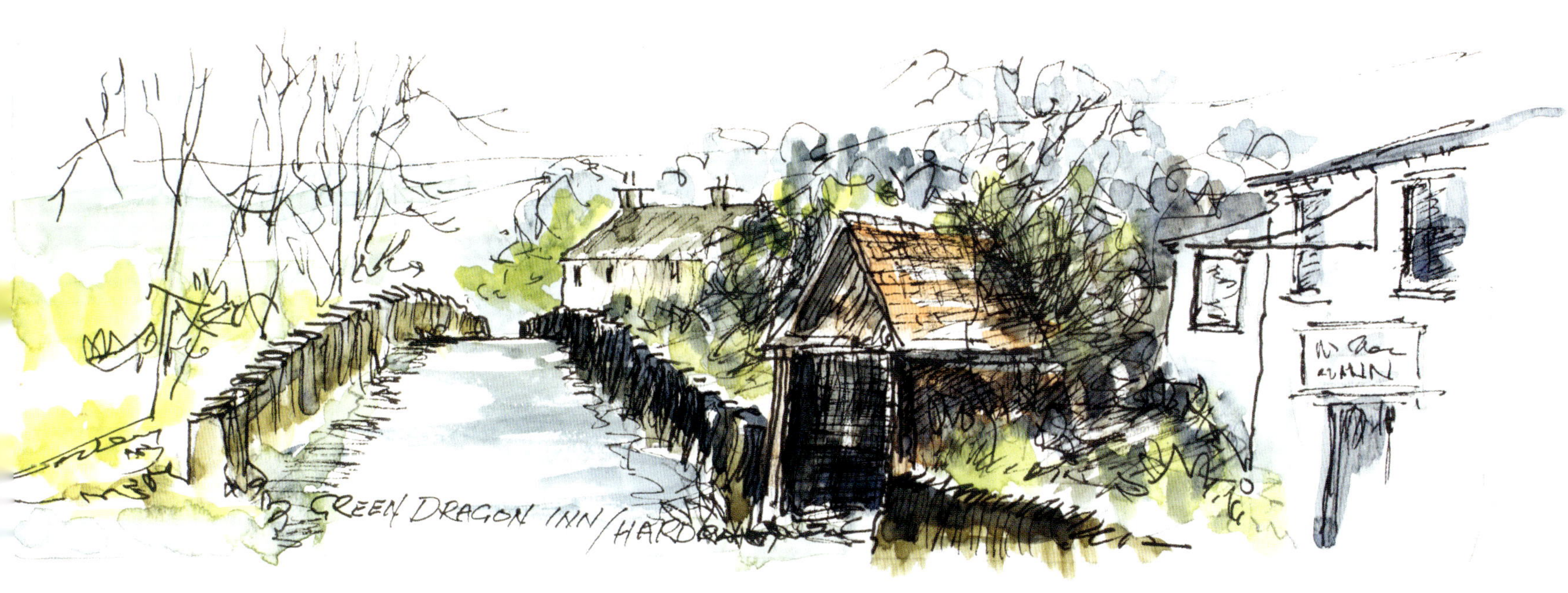

GREEN DRAGON INN/HARDRAW

Bridlington

The crisp blue of the sea and the sky belies the icy wind of the day, which the sailing boats are making good use of. Have you noticed how the red of the boats catches your eye before anything else? It reminds me of the time Turner repainted his painting on varnishing day, prior to the Summer Exhibition at The Royal Academy, London. He added a dot of bright red floating in a sea of grey to ensure people were captivated by his painting and not the ones to either side, one of which was Constable's, who had been working on his particular painting for thirteen years.

There is a little-known Harbour Museum which offers an insight into Bridlington, bringing its fishing history to life through interactive activities provided free of charge by volunteers. Hidden gems like this museum are often found when you are least looking.

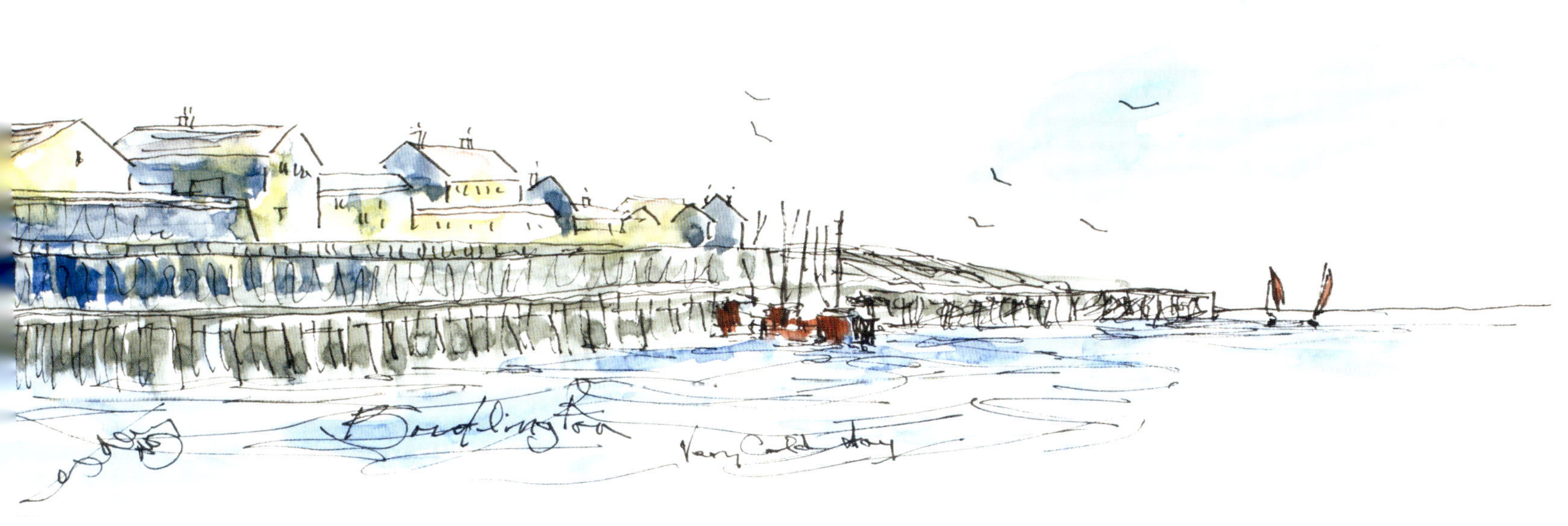
Bridlington
Very Cold day

Fat Betty

On Danby High Moor is 'Fat Betty'. Standing about 4 feet high, and what looks like a round shaped head with four indents resembling a face, this medieval cross has marked the path between Rosedale and Westerdale for centuries. It makes the hairs on the back of your neck stand up knowing that by following this moorland marker, you are following in the footsteps of others and adding your own footprints to hundreds of years of history.

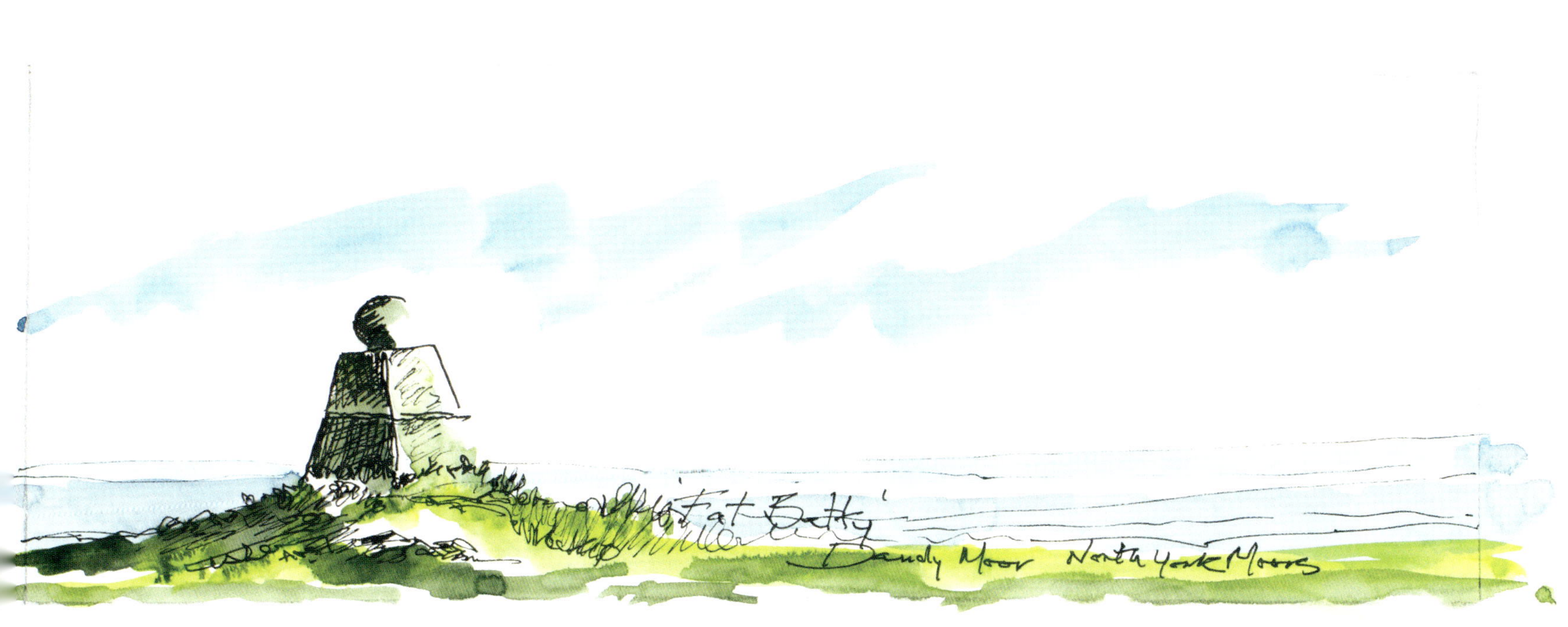
'Fat Betty'
Danby Moor   North York Moors

Penyghent

Penyghent is one of the Yorkshire Three Peaks, the other two being Ingleborough and Whernside. I have visited and climbed the peak many times, but not all days have been this clear (the cloud can often obscure the iconic landmark), however on this day I was lucky to capture the majestic landscape.

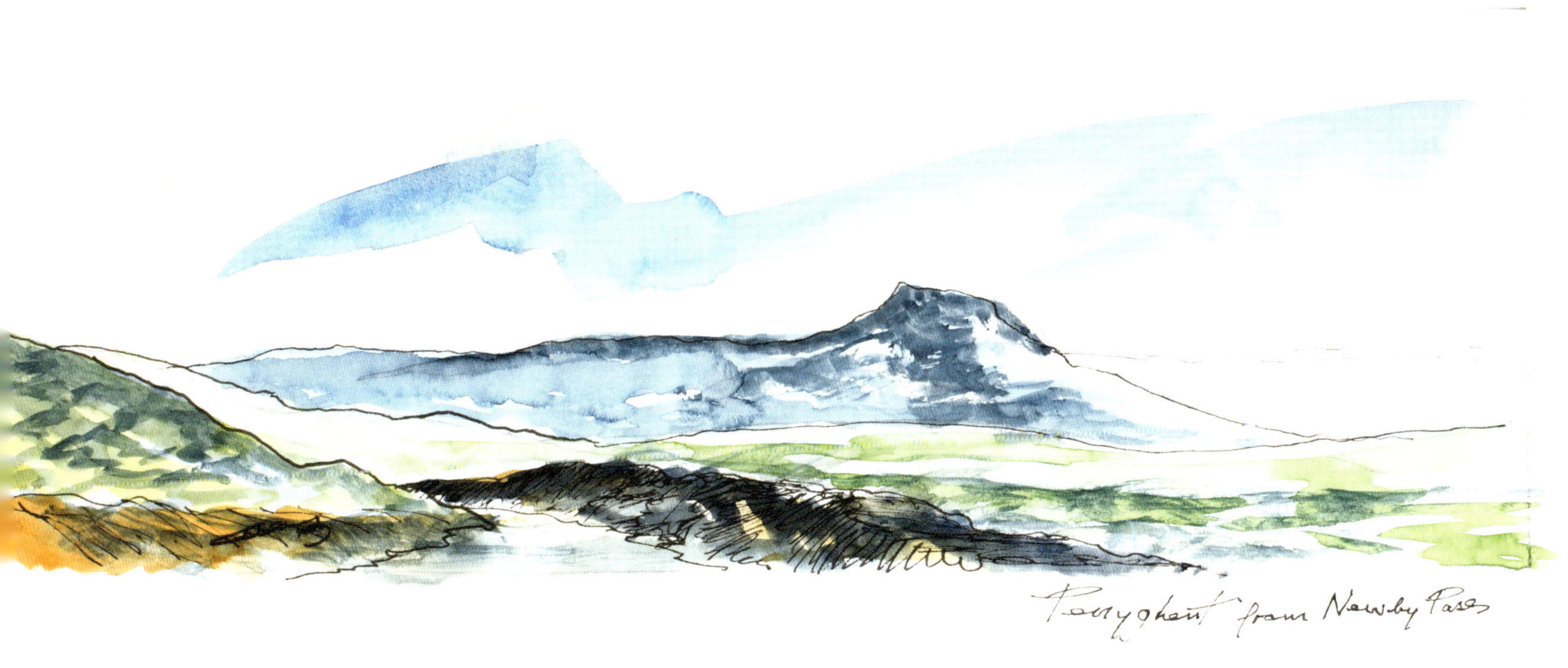
Penyghent from Newby Pass

Ribblehead Viaduct

You cannot fail to stand before Ribblehead Viaduct and not be in awe of what man can achieve. I know that I have mentioned its history before, but it would be hard not to stand in amazement of what the Victorians were able to construct without modern machinery. However, it was not completed without human cost; the graveyard in Chapel-le-Dale holds a memorial to all those who died during its construction.

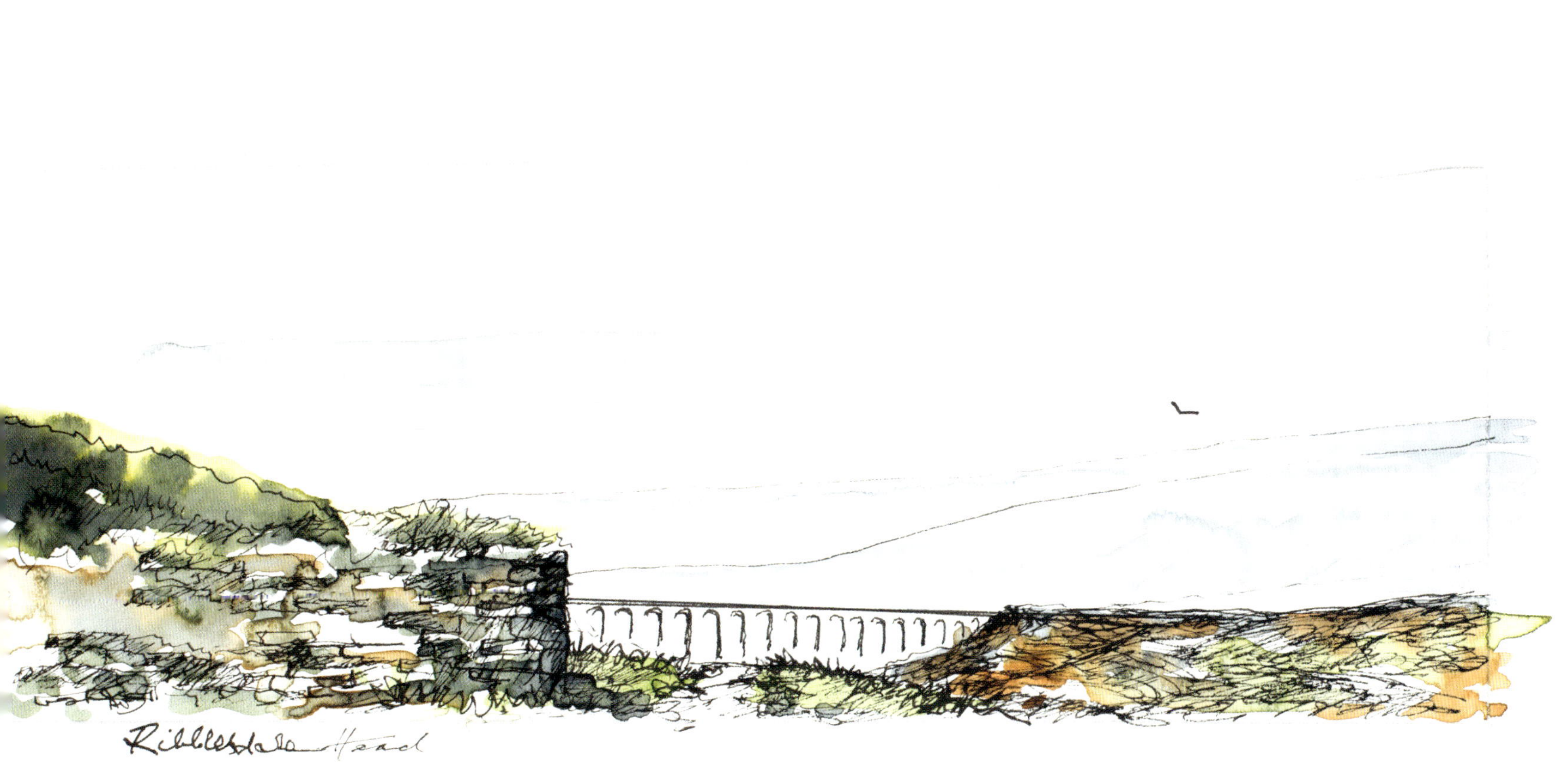

Ribblesdale Head

Colden, near Heptonstall

This sketch really gives you a feeling of the Brontes; in fact this area is called Bronte landscape. You can see the hard life that people had to survive; through the unforgiving winters, where there was no central heating, no transport and just the light of a candle. The poles you see on the right-hand side are electricity poles taking power into the hardest to reach locations.

The nearer I get to the upper moorlands, the closer I feel to my maker. Whether you say God or Mother Nature, this is where I feel most at home.

It reminds me very much of the words of John Newton: "I once was lost but now I'm found, was blind but now I see". When I stand upon the Yorkshire Moors I know I am right where I am meant to be.

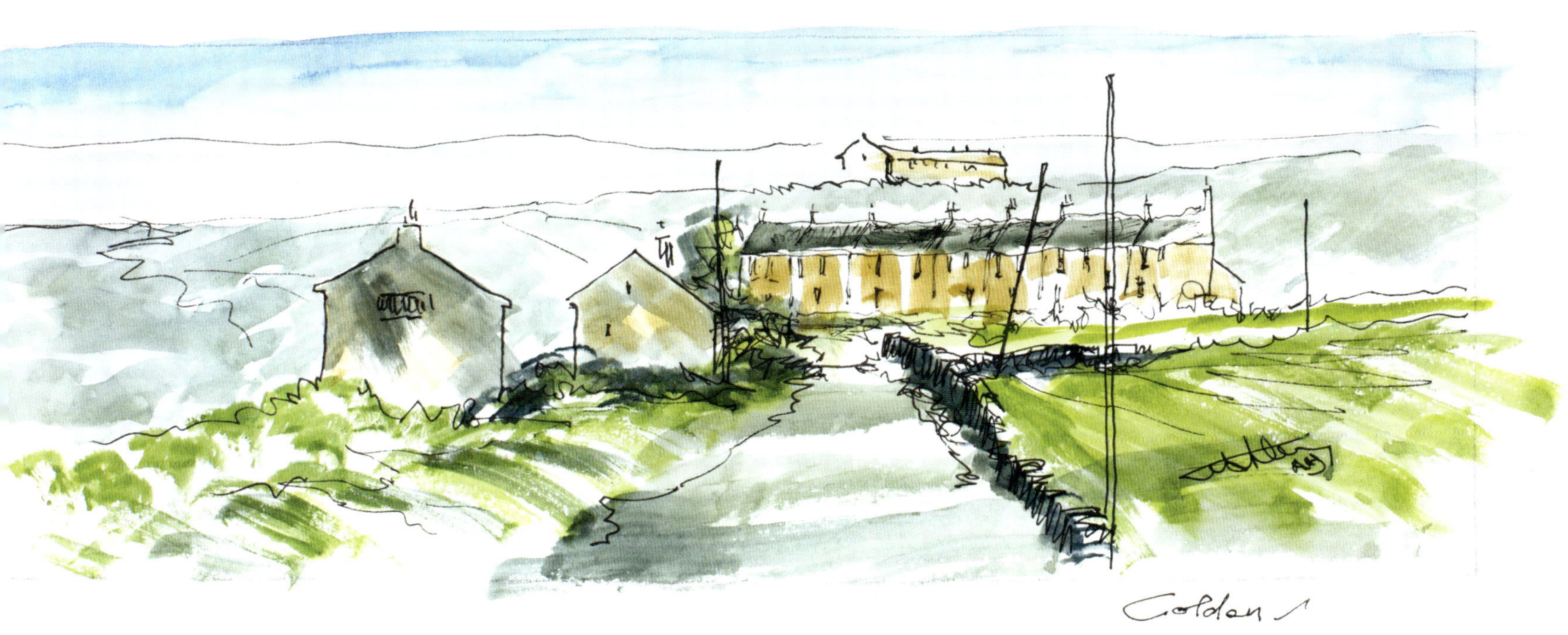

Colden, near Heptonstall   97

Buckden Bridge

The Grade II listed arches of Buckden Bridge span the river Wharfe, in the North Yorkshire district of Craven. If you are looking for a walk, the Yorkshire Dales National Park has a 4 mile circuit from Buckden to Cray to Hubberholme that takes in the bridge and the birds along the river bank.

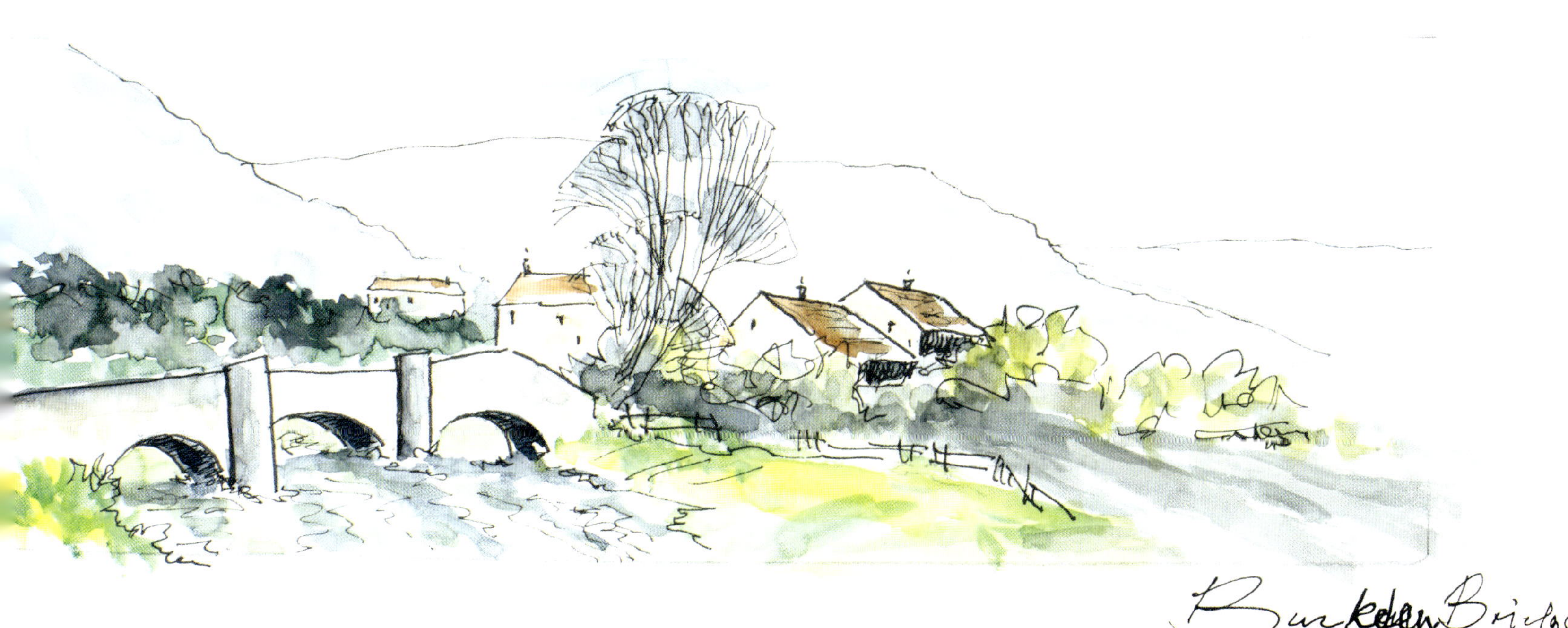
Buckden Bridge

Hill Top Ironworks, Rosedale

The great iron rush of the 1850s lasted a surprisingly long time, with the tranquil moorland uplands being traversed by railway lines, mines, blast furnaces and settlements, the remnants of which can still be seen today.

As open mining and imports became more cost effective, the North Yorkshire mines could no longer keep up with demand and by the Second World War, the mining of the moors was over, leaving only its historical mark upon the landscape.

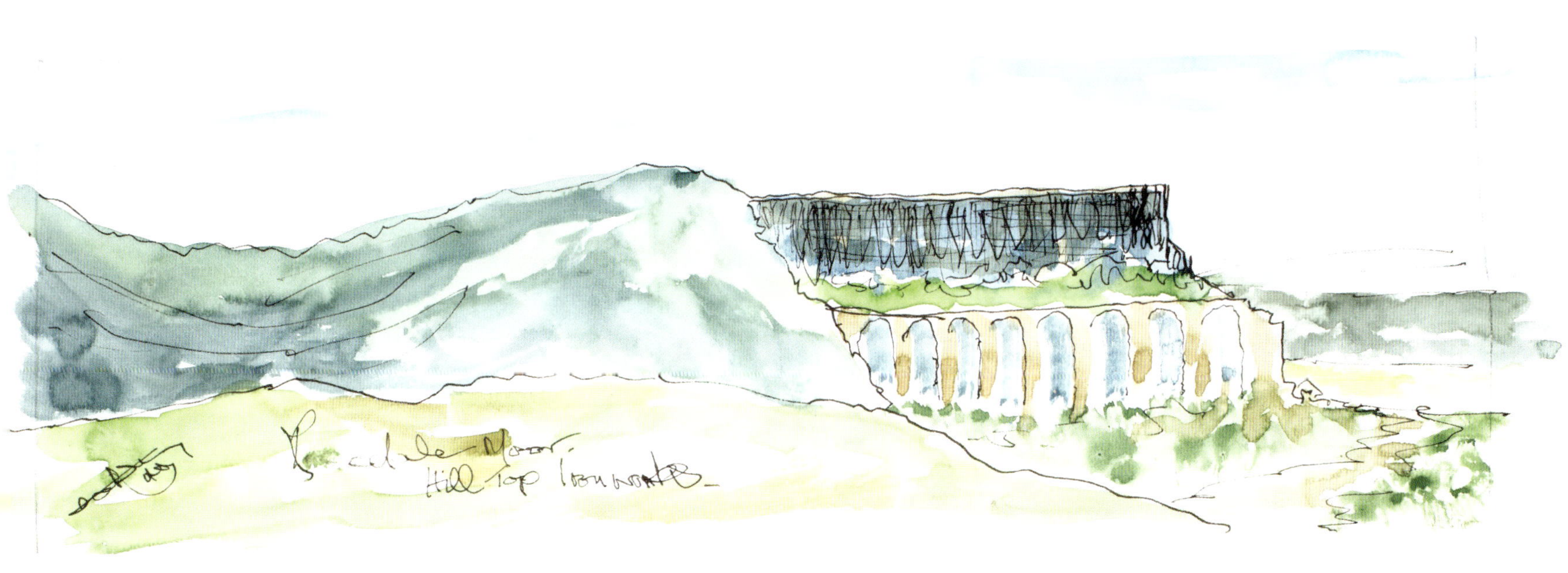
Rosedale Moor
Hill Top Ironworks

Roseberry Topping Standing Stones, Danby Moor

Standing on Danby Moor, it was such a clear day that it appeared as if the earth had opened up beneath my feet and the miles between the standing stone and Roseberry Topping appeared to reduce before my eyes.

These are the days that you could stand for hours and just soak in the landscape, allowing it to seep under your skin and be absorbed by all your senses.

"Heaven is under our feet as well as over our heads." H. D. Thoreau

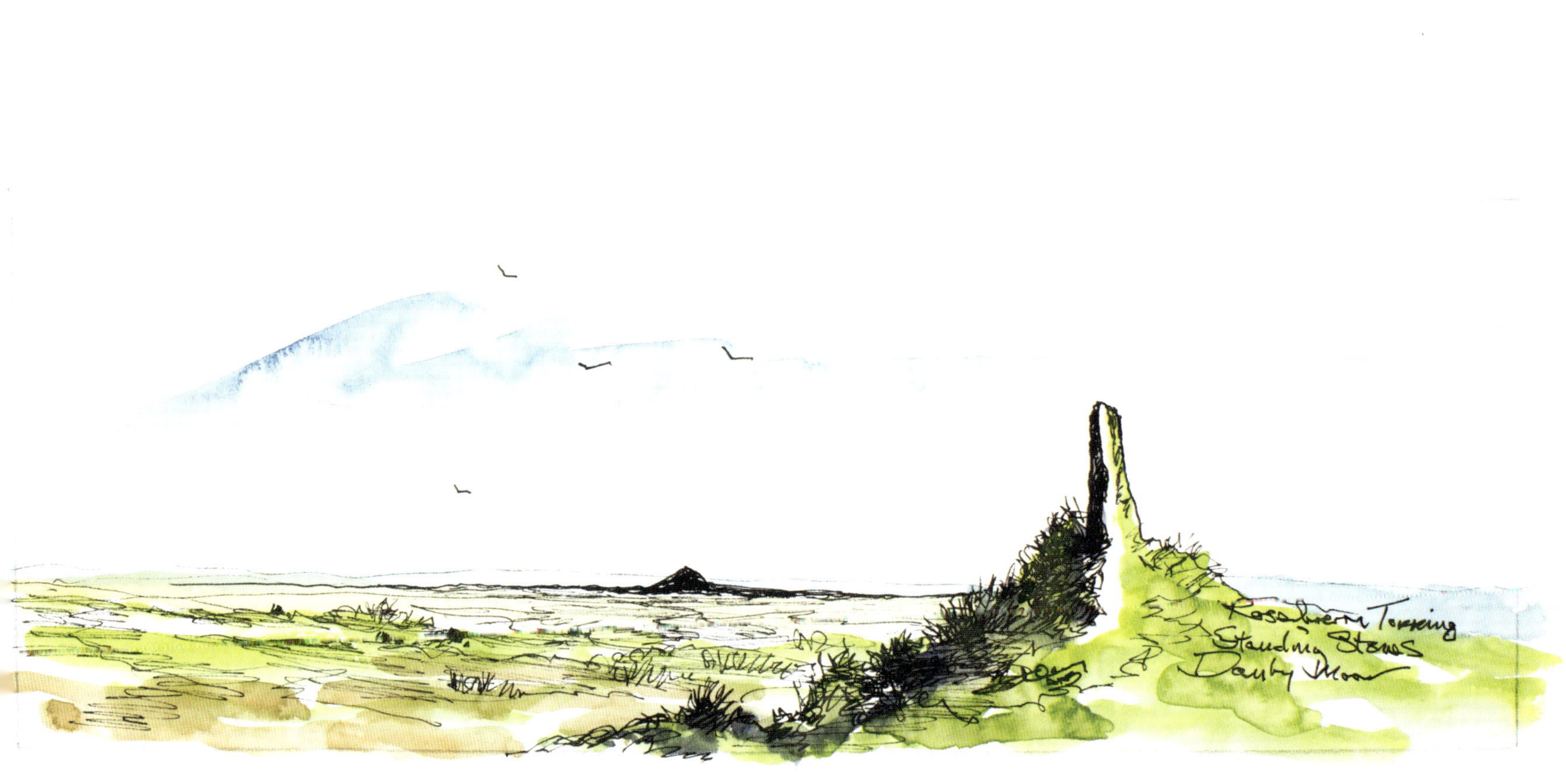

Roseberry Topping
Standing Stones
Danby Moor

Kidstone Pass

The beauty of Buckden is that from this location you can go up to Kidstone Pass, Buckden Pike or over the road to Hawes and see some mind-blowing scenery. Wharfedale is a tranquil dale in the winter, but a popular visitor location during the summer, so if you like solitude then wait until later in the year. On this day I chose Kidstone Pass, which connects Buckden and Cray in upper Wharfedale with Bishopdale and Wensleydale.

What I enjoy about nature is that it is often self-explanatory; it is quite evident which way the wind blows, and if we stop for a minute, we see so much more than first impressions.

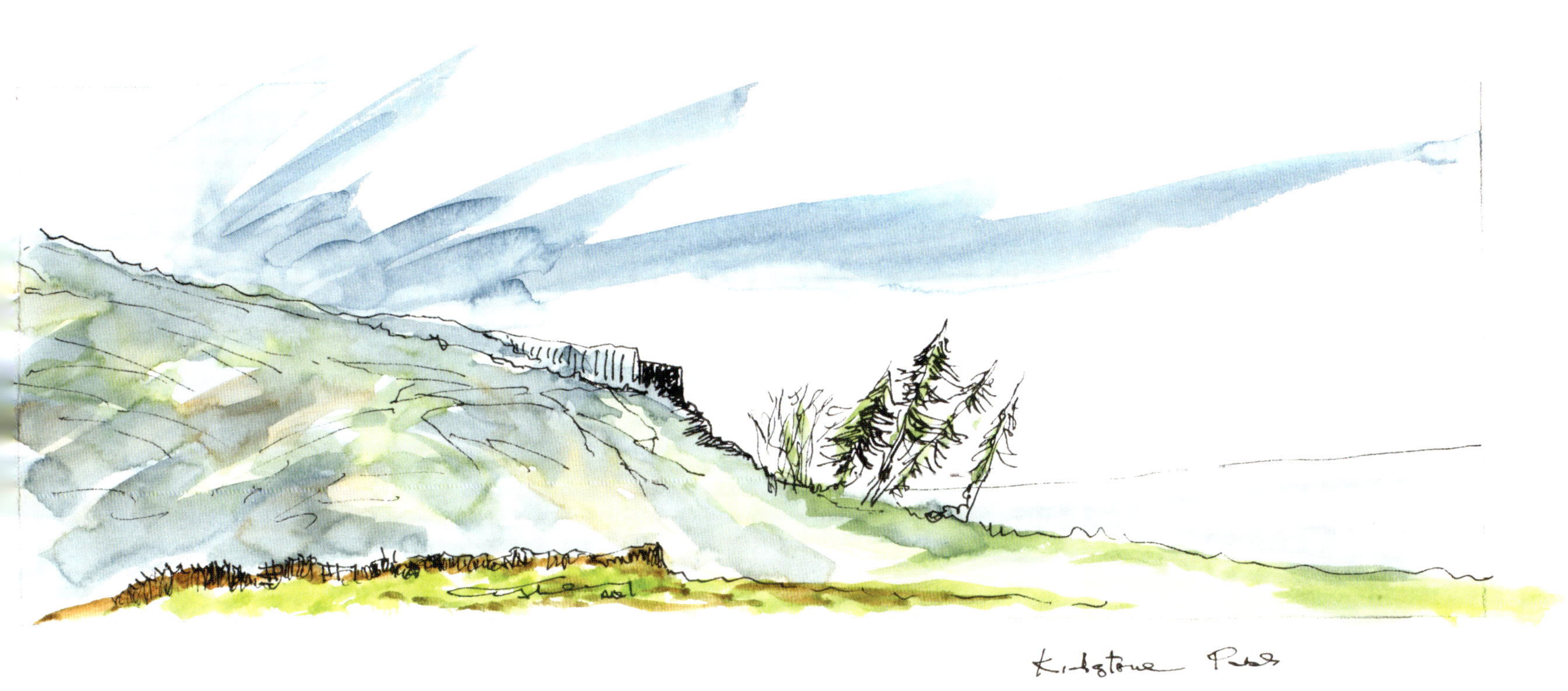

Newby Head Pass

At 439 metres above sea level, Newby Head Pass is so named after the Drovers Inn at Newby Head, and travels between Hawes and Ingleton. It is an experience to drive it in the summer, with its curves and panoramic views, but be warned not to attempt it through the winter months when snow is on the ground, as it is an exposed road open to the elements.

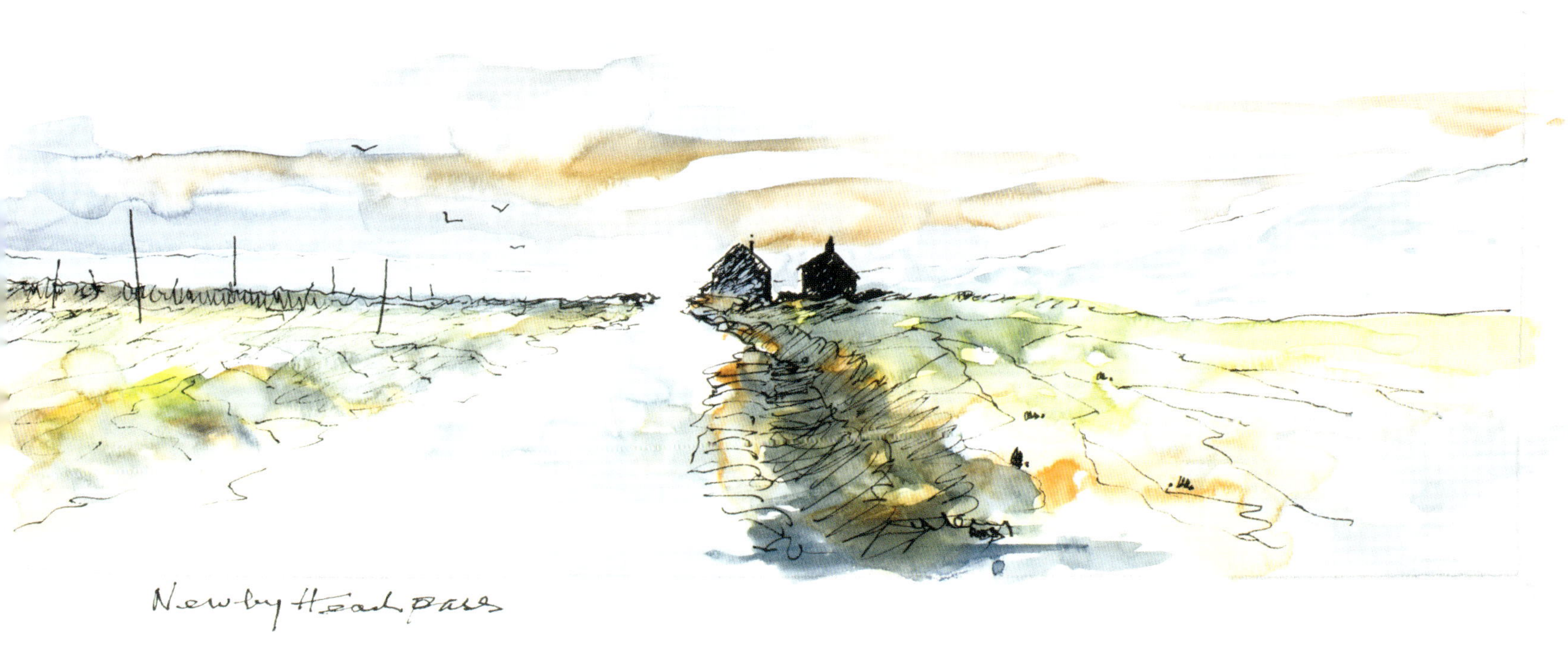

Newby Head Pass

Hawnby Hill

On first sight this could be mistaken for Roseberry Topping, but if you look closely, its smoother less craggy shape gives it away; this is Hawnby Hill.

The B1257 from Helmsley was just a panorama for the soul that day, filled with warmth and colour from the heather moorland, the woodland in the middle distance and then the majestic hills rising out of the moorland. From an artist's point of view, nothing more could be desired for composition and nature had provided it.

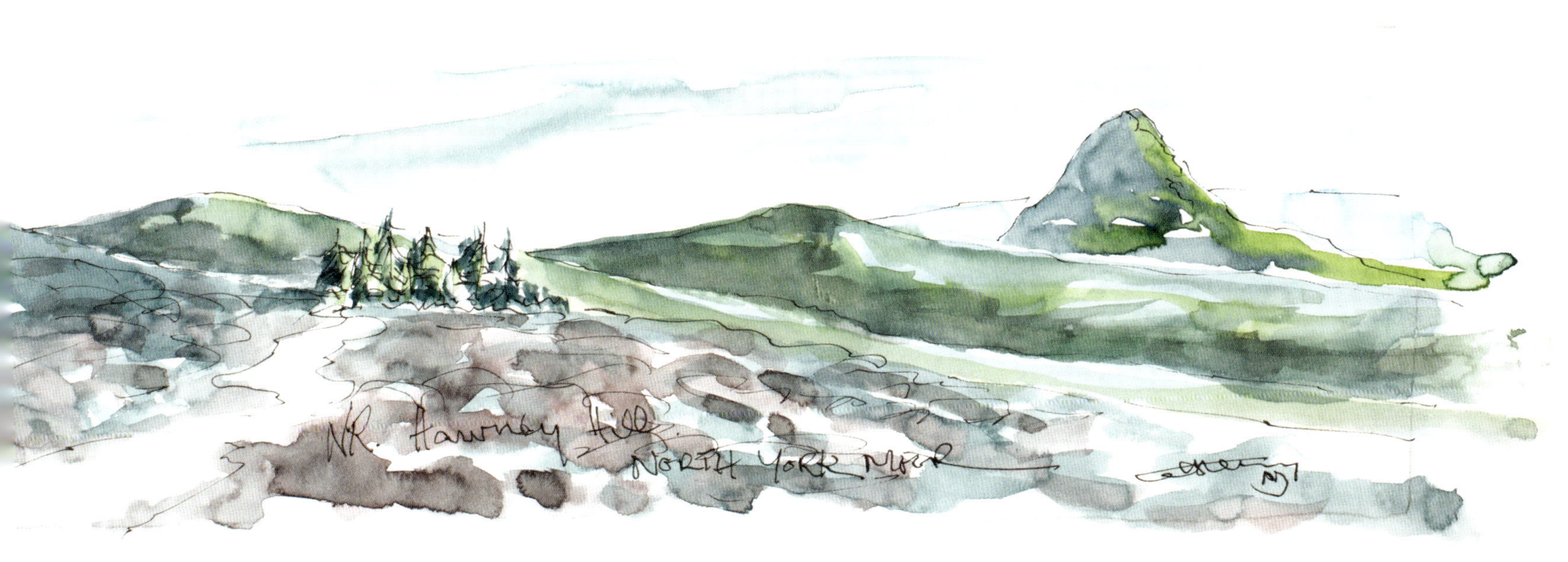

NR. Hawnby Hill.
NORTH YORK MOOR

Muker

Muker is a popular destination for walkers, being on the path of both the Pennine Way and the Coast to Coast walks. Built on a hillside above the river Swale, it has everything that you would wish for in a small village, as well as the peace of the Swaledale landscape for you to lose yourself in. Take your walking boots and escape the fast pace of life for an afternoon or weekend.

I wanted to include the sketch of 'Down to Muker' so that you could see that there is solitude to be found.

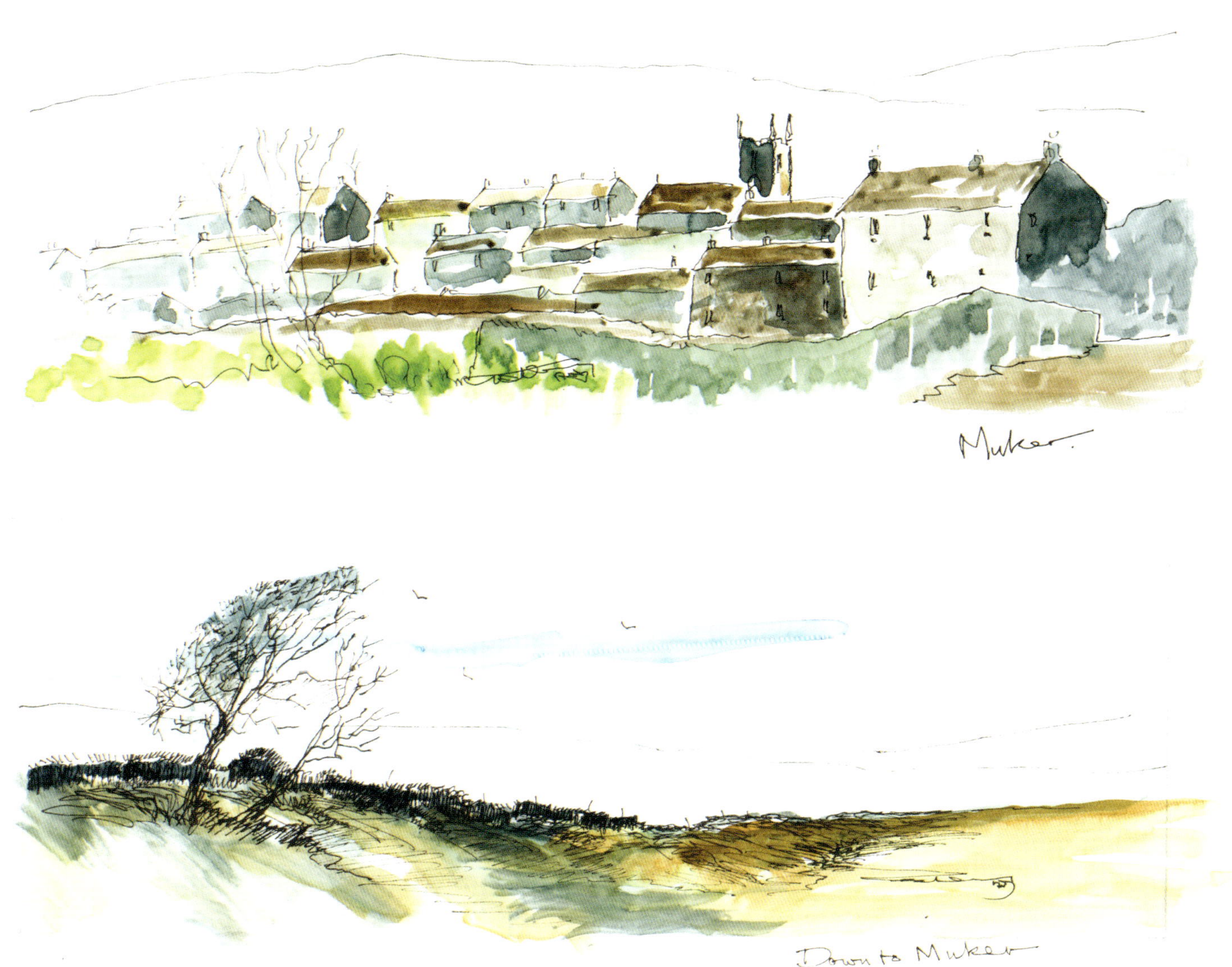

Muker.

Down to Muker

From Tan Hill into Swaledale and Over to Wensleydale

Here the blue skies with birds in flight are misleading. I always talk about man's ability to live alongside nature, particularly those who live off the land, and how hard the landscape can be; one moment it is your friend and the next it can be as harsh as a winter's gale. To live on the moors is to respect the weather and be able to read its subtle signs of change, such as the drop in atmospheric pressure, the changing light, or the way the trees are blown, and be able to steer your livestock through the storm.

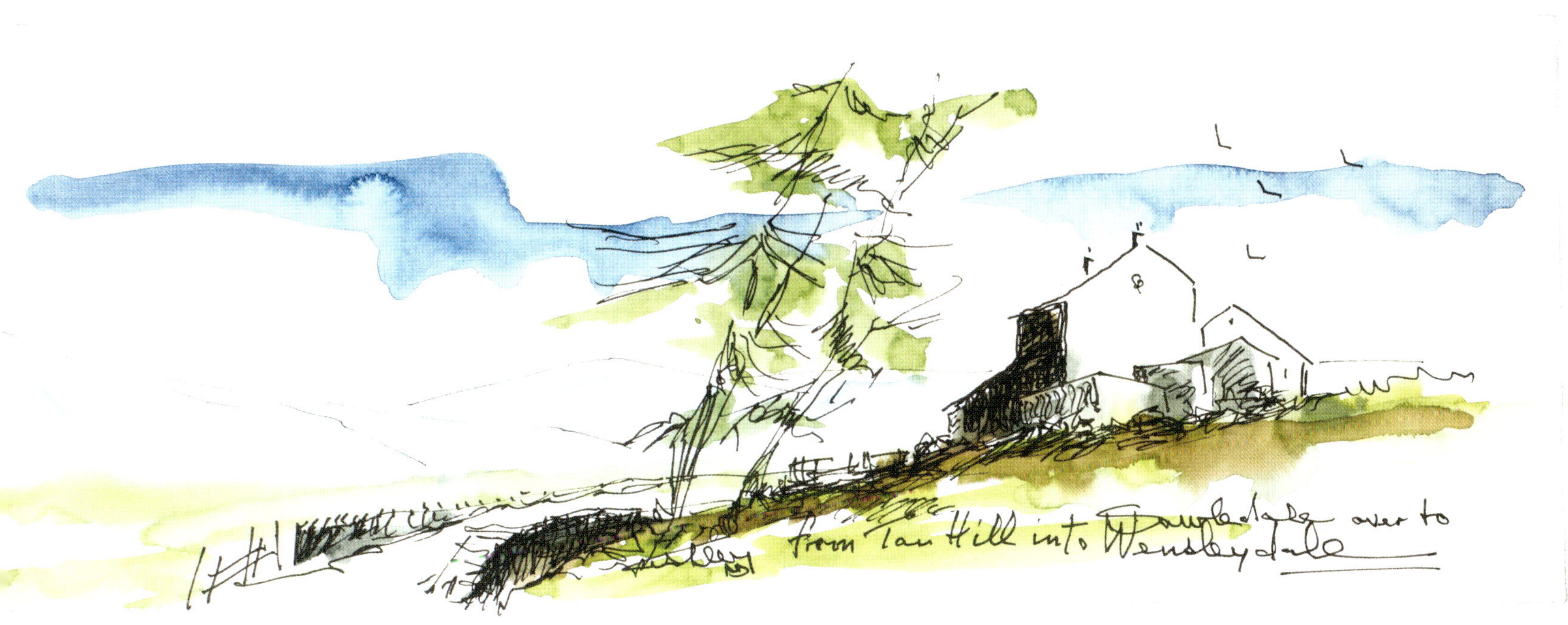
From Tan Hill into Wensleydale

Kilnsey Crag

The imposing lion's head of Kilnsey Crag is iconic. Once seen it is never forgotten, and it is one of my favourite sculptures by Mother Nature herself, with the limestone overhang having been carved by the Wharfedale glacier in the Ice Age.

From following in the footsteps of JMW Turner with the ITV Calendar News team, to taking my young grandchildren to the trout farm, each visit holds a special memory for me that will hopefully not be eroded by time.

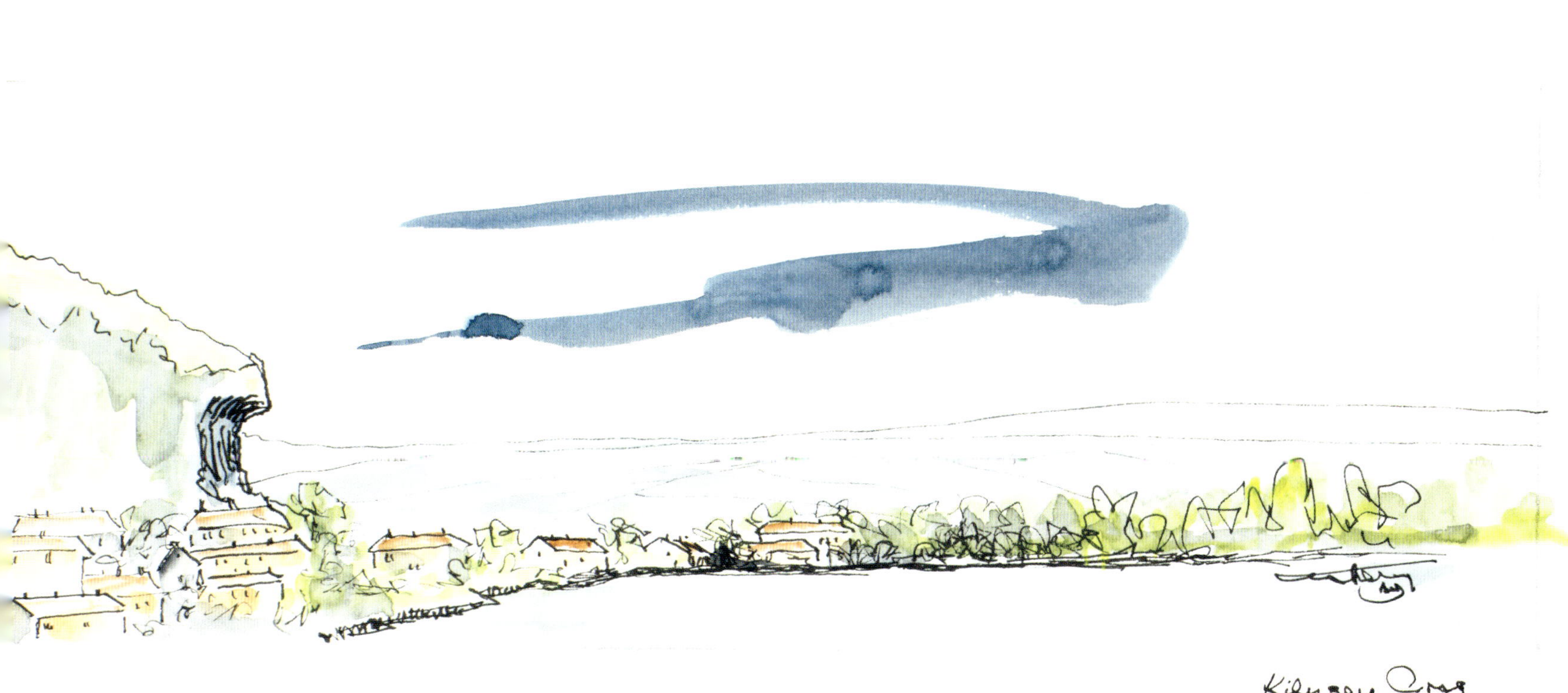

Kilnsey Crag   115

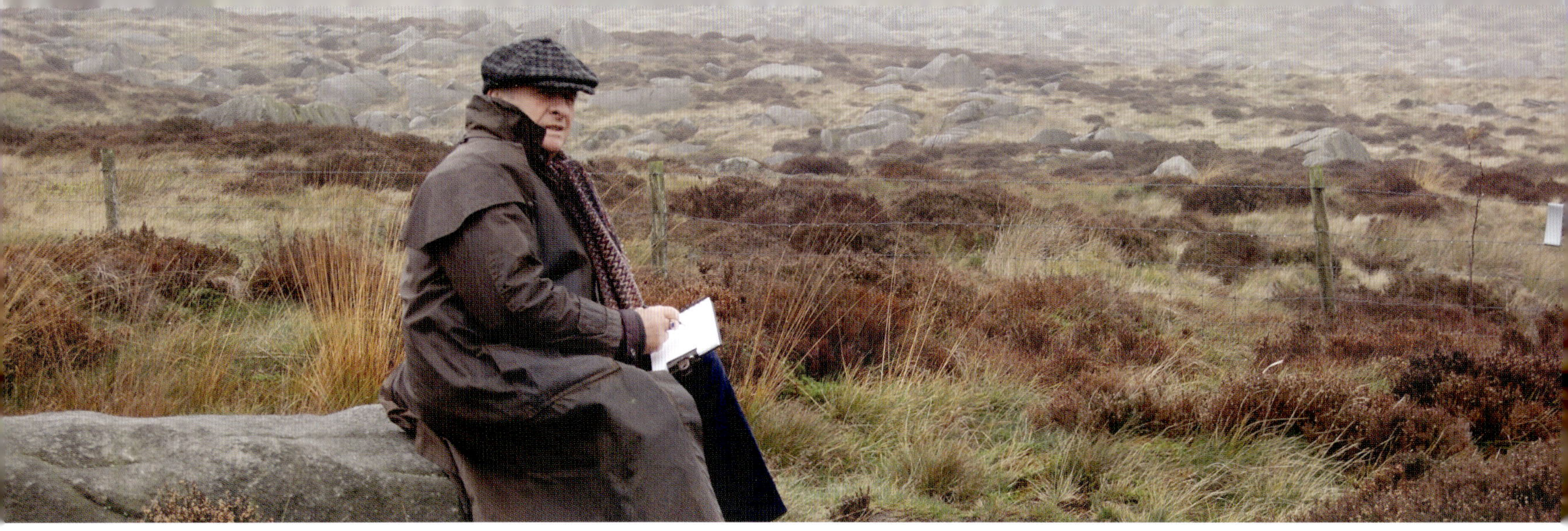

Marsden Moor

If you ever wish to escape from the worries and fast pace of everyday life, this is the place to go. It is my personal go to ....come rain or shine the landscape provides a warm embrace. Autumn is sublime with the contrast of the burnt sienna moorland against the crisp, cobalt-blue sky. Take a moment to close your eyes and listen to nature, the wind followed by the cries of the lapwing and curlew. Then re open your eyes and absorb the colours, it truly fills the heart and calms the mind. Here I am at peace with the world.

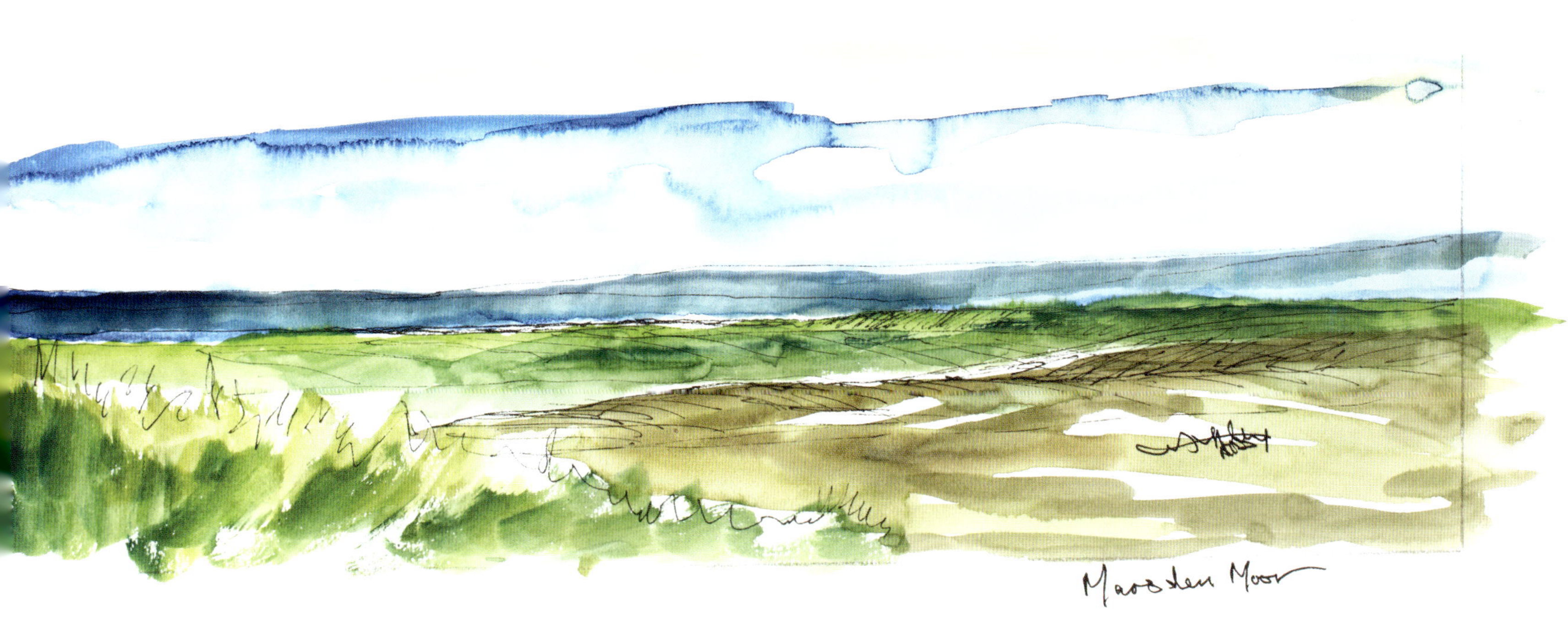

Marsden Moor

Holme Moss to Castle Hill

The term 'head in the clouds' reminds me of Holme Moss, as it offers a vantage point across the whole of the Holme Valley and further on a good day, but choose a day with low cloud and you will barely see 100 metres in front of you.

At the top of Holme Moss is a viewing car park and to the left–hand side off the road is a 'Framing the landscape ' frame, sponsored by the University of Huddersfield. If you are getting out of your car to view please hold on tightly to the handle when you open the door, as the wind is notorious at whipping it out of your hand and causing major crumpling of your metal work. Nature is definitely a fierce opponent on this exposed landscape, but should you wish to take up the challenge, the view can be awe inspiring.

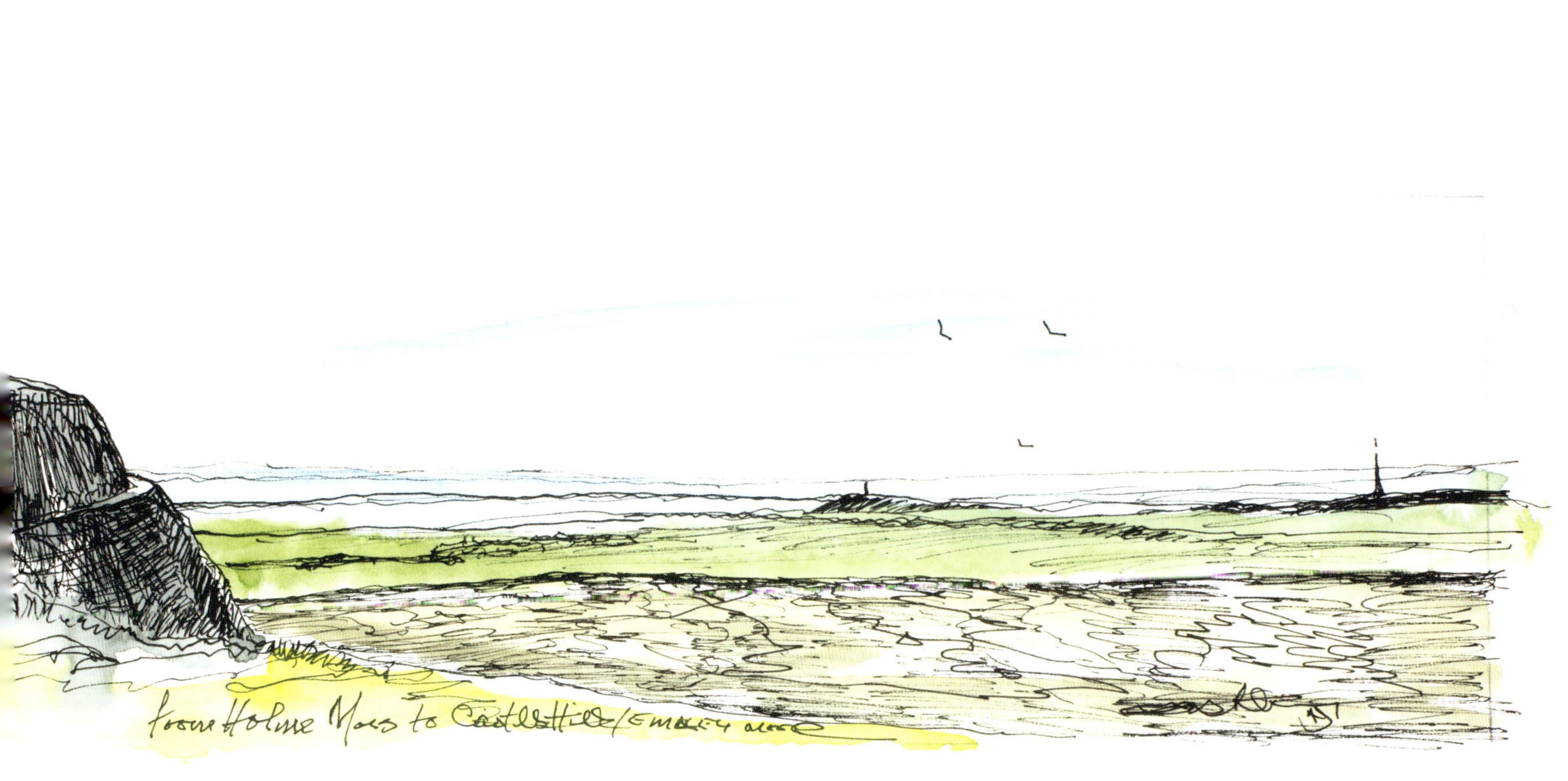
from Holme Moss to Castle Hill / Emley aerial

Stoodley Pike from Blackshaw Edge

Stoodley Pike can clearly be seen in the distance. Like Castle Hill is to the Holme Valley, the monument to the fallen of the Crimean War is the same to Calderdale; it is a lighthouse to navigate homeward through the frozen seas. A point of reference to the eye and to the heart.

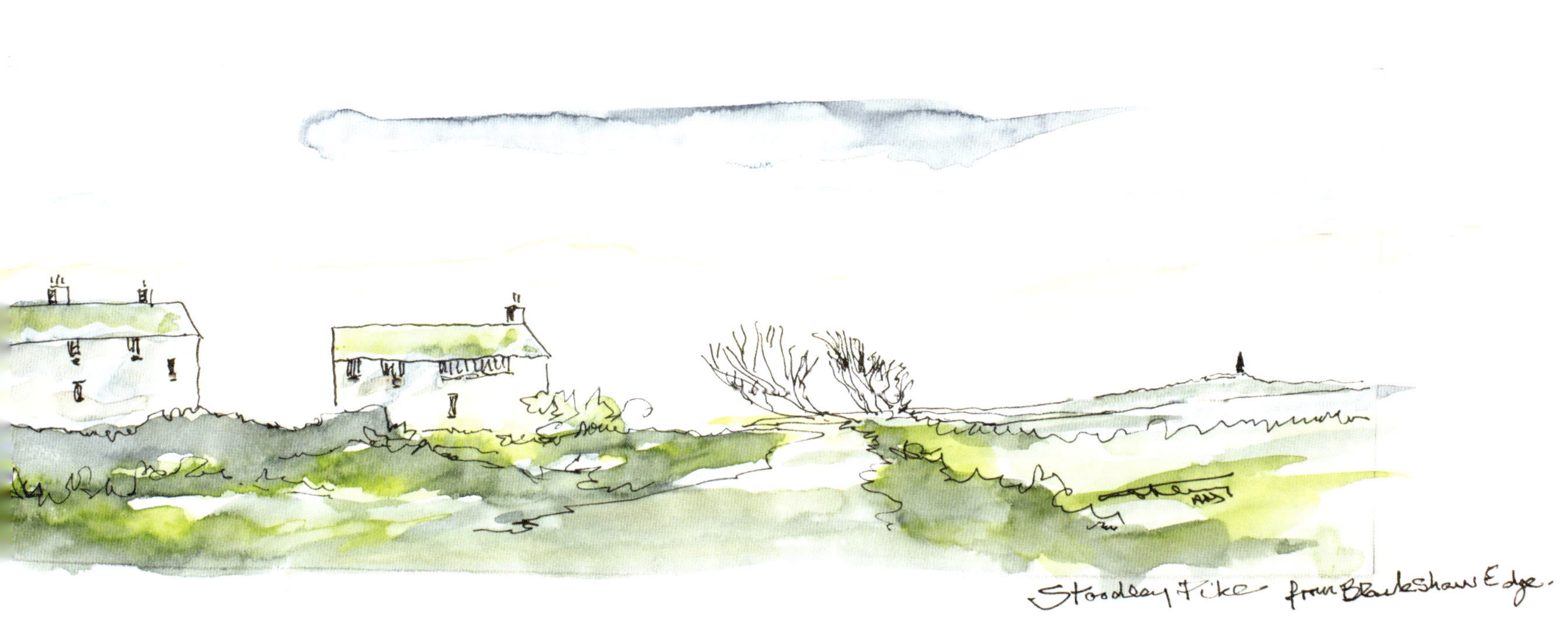

Stoodley Pike from Blackshaw Edge   121

Fremington Edge on the Road to Tan Hill

The farm sits in total isolation; exposed to the elements with a small bridge crossing a stream. Although an icy day, the kind when your head hurts from the cold, it allowed the sunlight to highlight the moorland, as if a stream of light was finding its way like a torch illuminating the green. The cloud firmly sits over the middle distance, casting its blue shadow over the farm house.

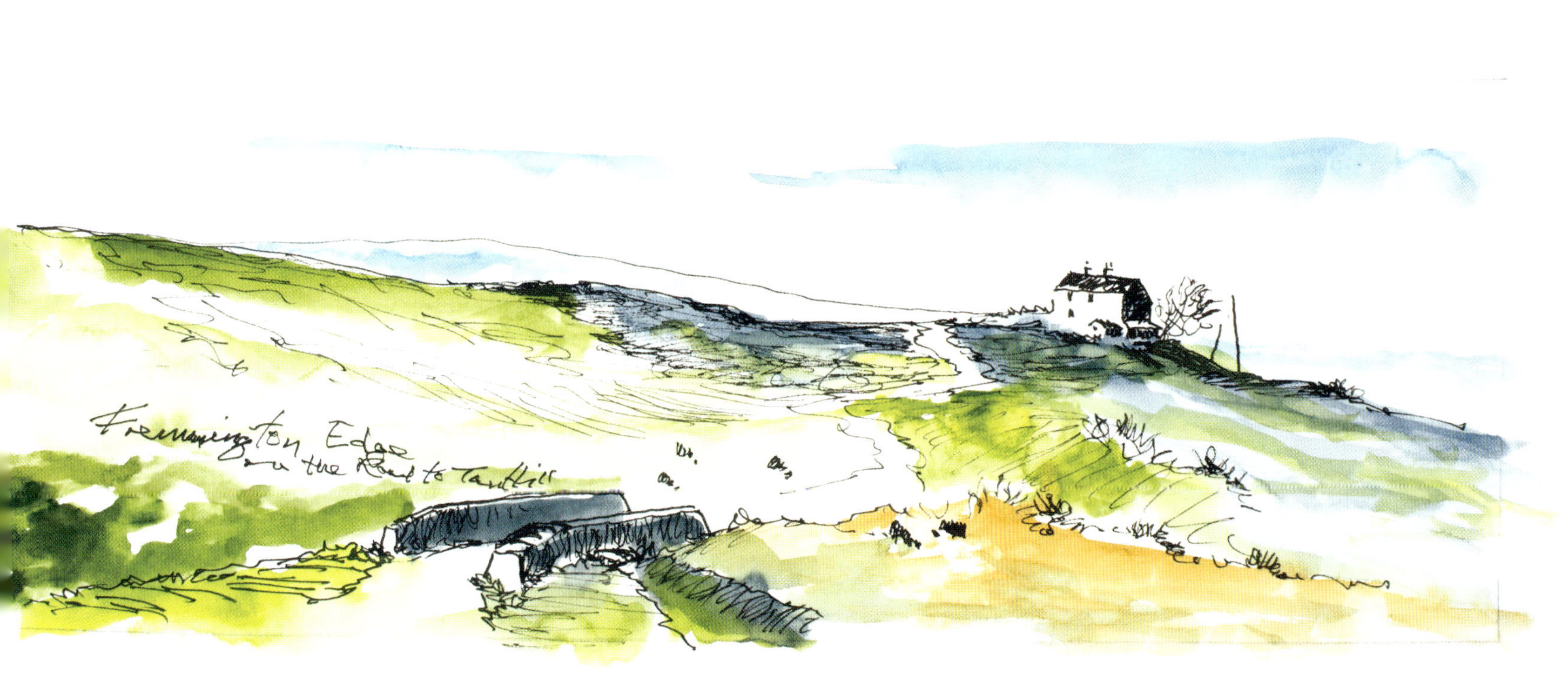
Fremington Edge
on the Road to Tan Hill

Black Dyke,
Blackshaw Edge

This is a hidden gem that is underestimated as a destination. Calderdale gives me the feeling of 'Wuthering Heights' and is completely different to anywhere else in Yorkshire. The Yorkshire landscape has been many an inspiration for poets, writers, artists and composers, thus I am not alone in feeling the pulse of Yorkshire flowing through my veins, for it has captured my soul for eternity.

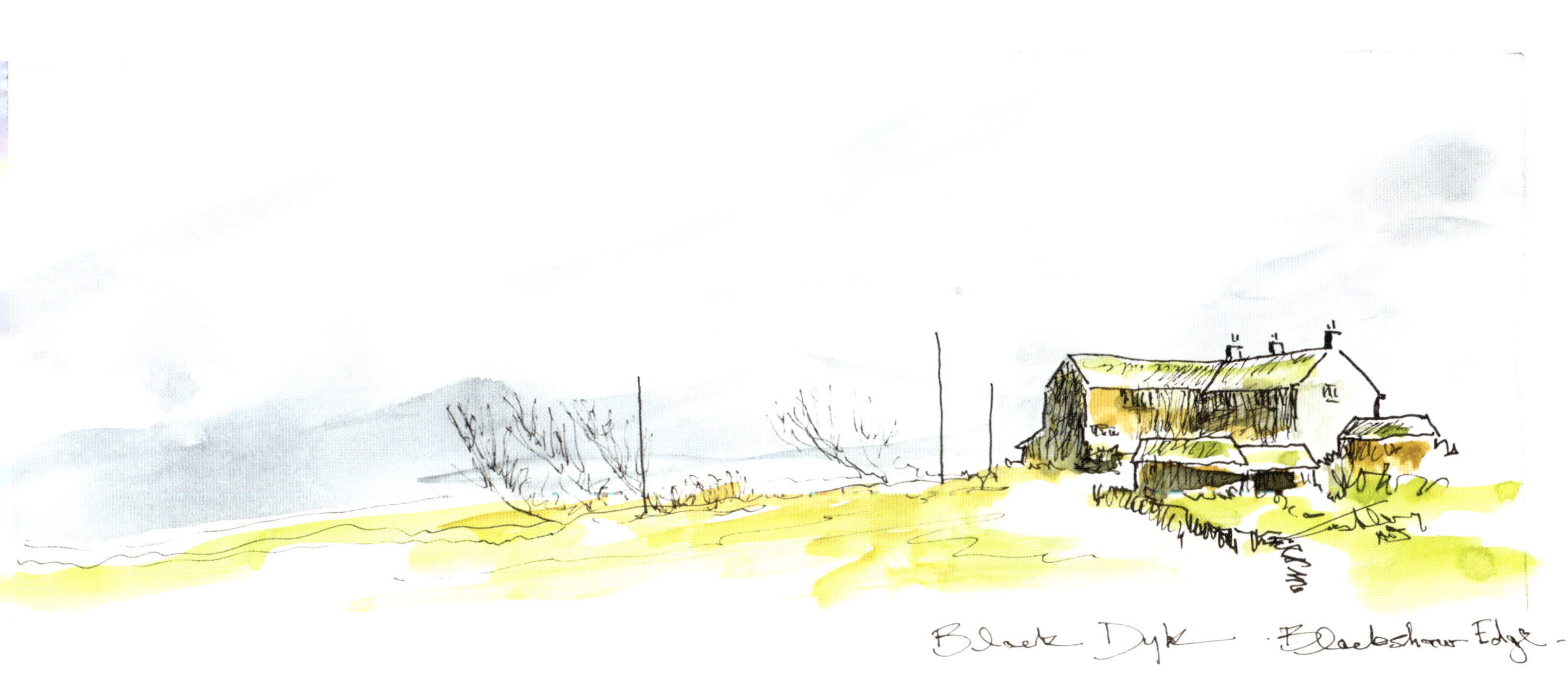
Black Dyke · Blackshaw Edge ·

Worton, Wensleydale

When I paint I enjoy the solitude, the time to lose myself in the moment. It is completely different when I sketch. Often I am happy to have the company and on this day my wife, Anne, was with me. It reminds me of the camping trips we took in our first years of marriage. It makes me smile now because if you can laugh through the wind and rain whilst sat in a water-logged tent, I think you can withstand anything... needless to say we have been married for over fifty-six years.

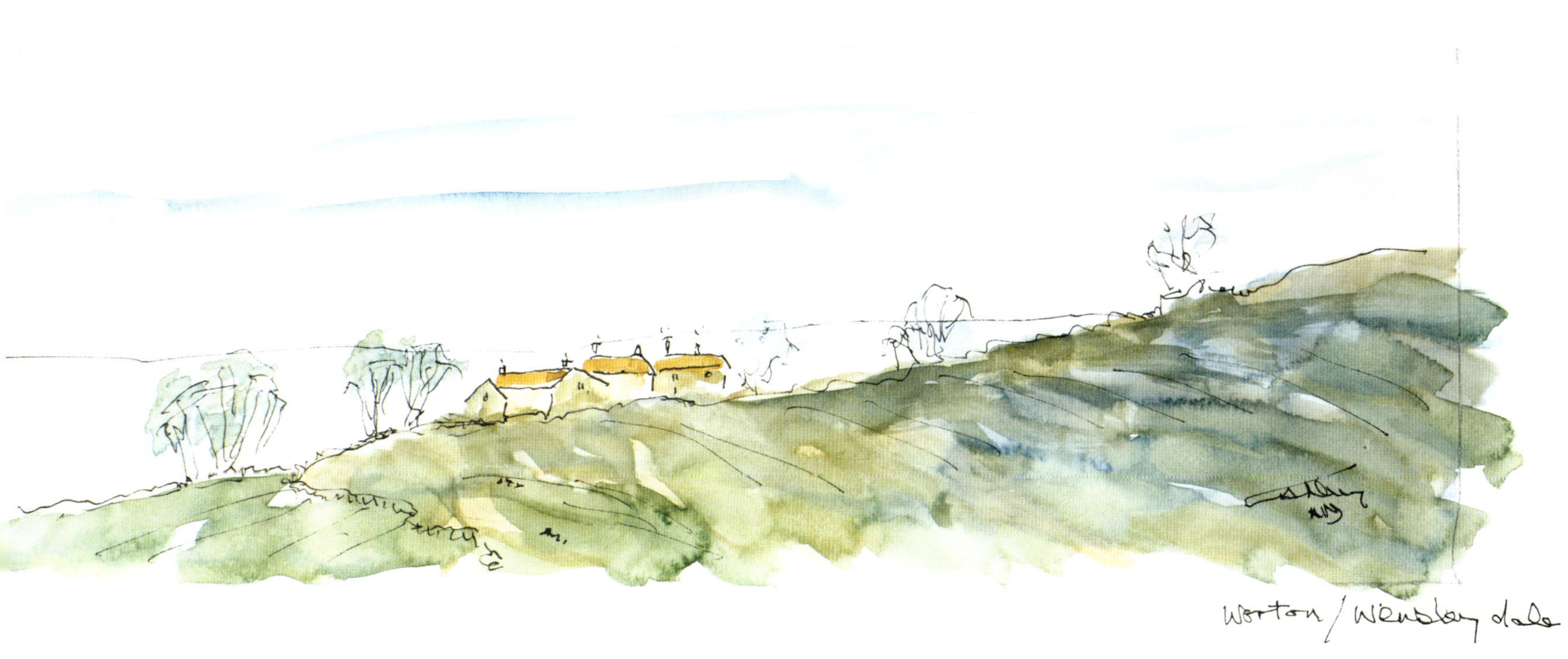

Worton, Wensleydale   127

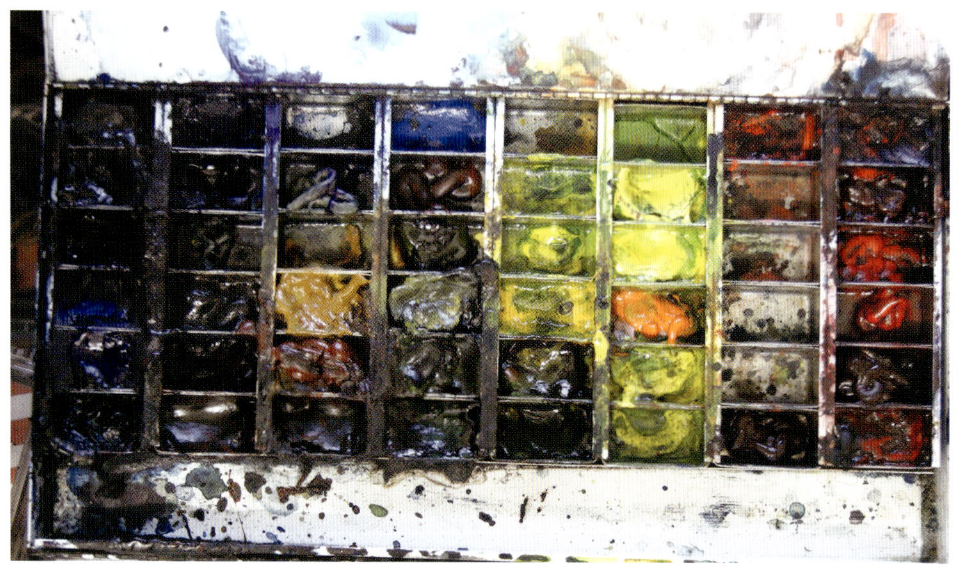

Wensleydale

The wall and gatepost signify man's mark on the landscape; slotted together like pieces of a jigsaw, the individual fields are marked out along the landscape. Often gateposts can be found on the open moor, standing upright like gravestones. A tribute to lives gone by that worked and lived on the land, they are all that remain of the boundary walls.

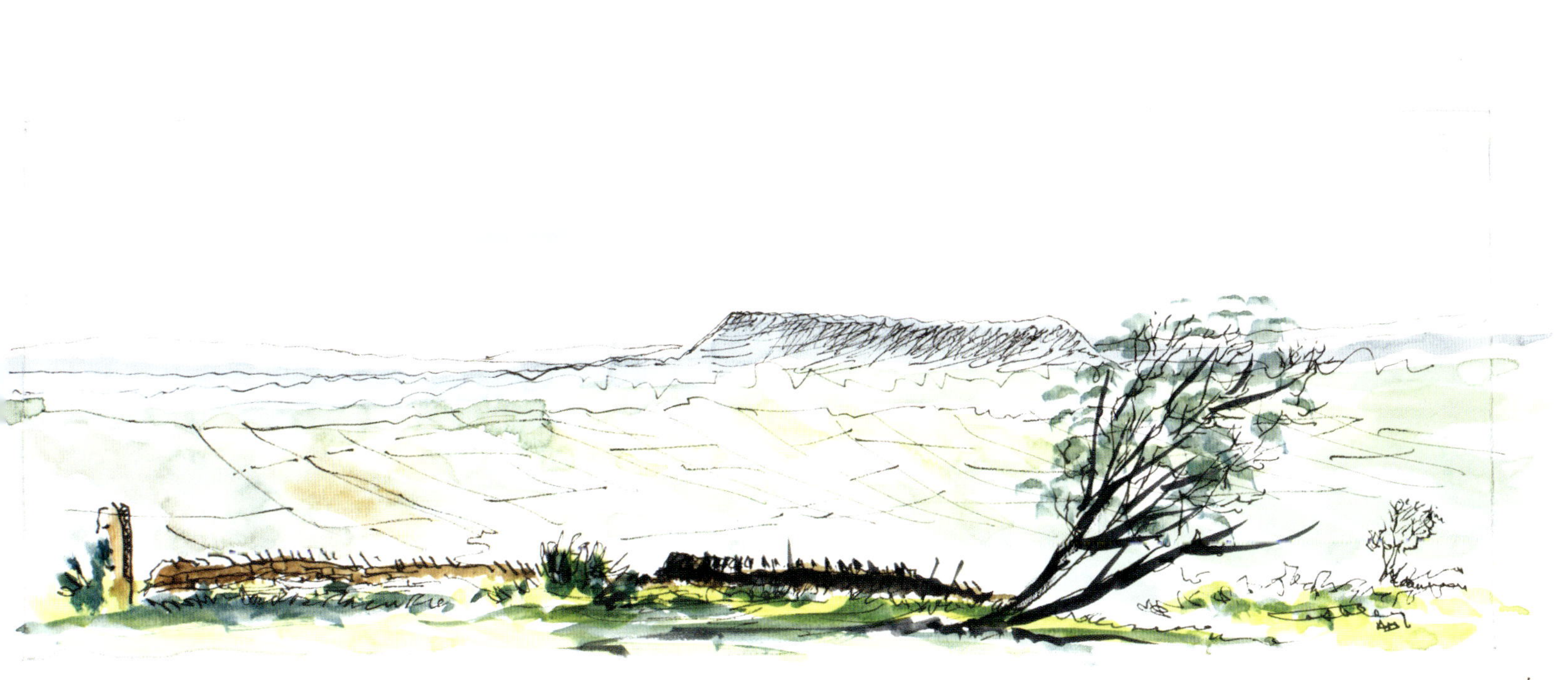

Wensleydale Near Leyburn

Pecket Well

Above Hebden Bridge is Pecket Well. A mill was opened here in 1858 and was the last faustian-weaving mill in Hebden Bridge when it closed in 1998. It has now been converted into dwellings and the mill, engine house, chimney and weaving shed, which were built between 1840 and 1858, are now listed buildings. I often wonder whether the new inhabitants hear the sound of workers' clogs in the dead of the night. I think it is fantastic that a new use has been found whilst preserving its heritage. I know time moves on, but we should also retain historical buildings wherever possible.

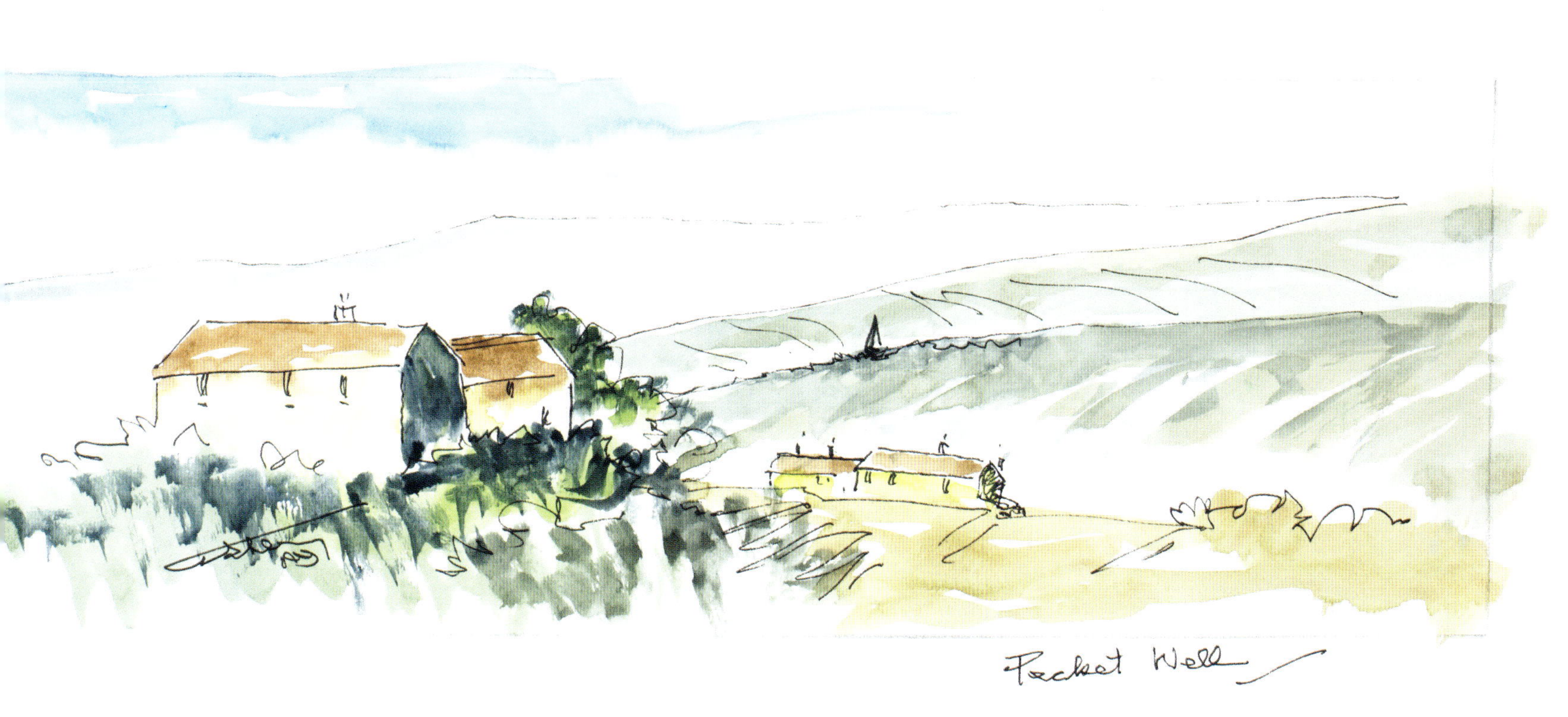

Fremington Edge, near Reeth

Found north of the village of Reeth, in Swaledale, the limestone crags of Fremington Edge join Arkengarthdale to Swaledale. Here it can be seen as a dramatic backdrop to the farm house. Those of you who have viewed my paintings will know that I am captivated by the atmospheric skies of Yorkshire, but as this was a clear day it was the stark limestone that was to act as the contrast to the soft landscape in the foreground.

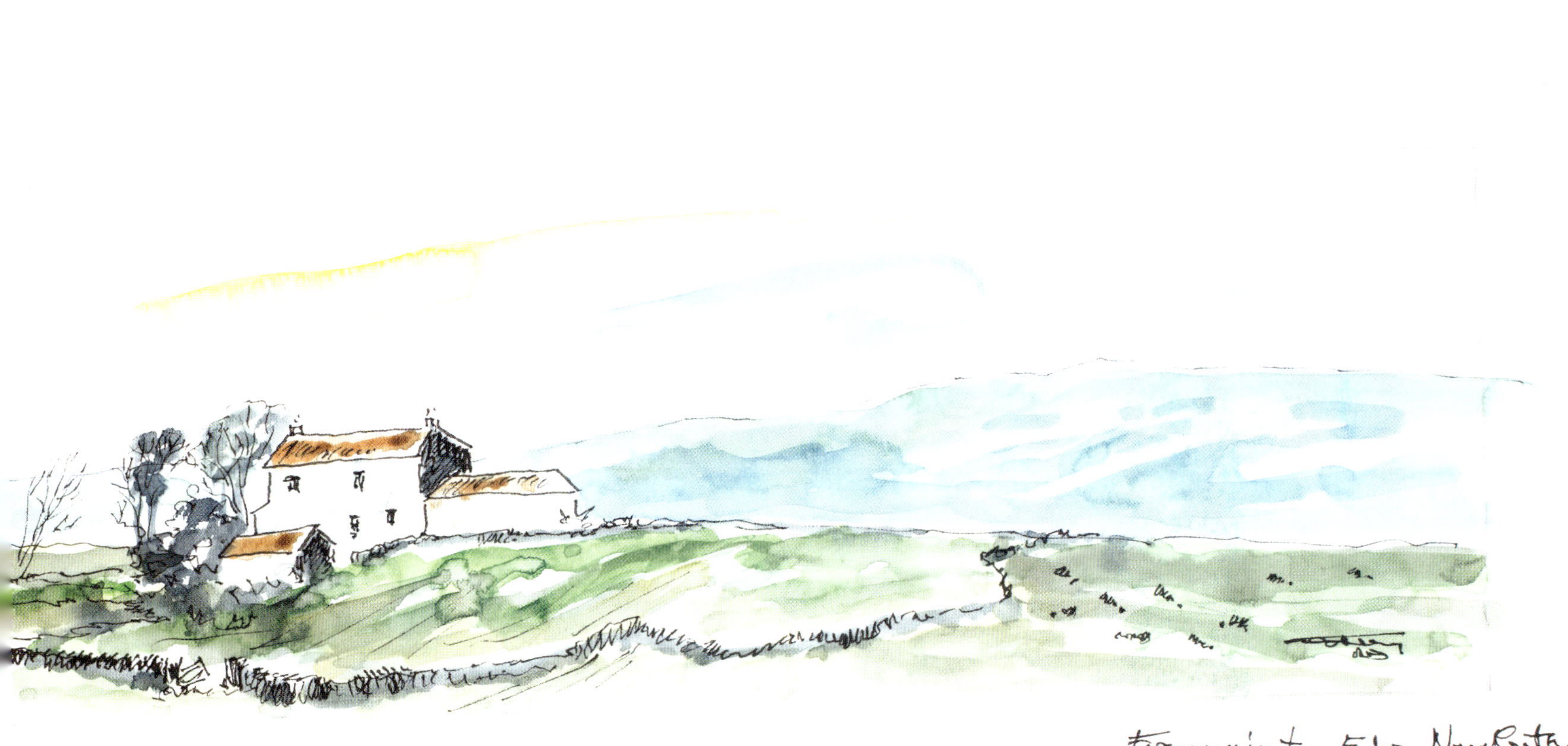

Fremington Edge, near Reeth   133

Colne Road, Hebden Bridge

I cannot help but look at the terraced row up on the exposed Colne Road above Hebden Bridge and think of the term 'brace yourself', for that is what the houses appear to be doing; standing tall together against whatever nature may throw at its inhabitants. They have been built to survive.

A slight mental detour, but if you are passing by Halifax to visit Hebden Bridge take time to visit the recently renovated Piece Hall, which was originally built for people to trade their textiles. As part of Yorkshire's heritage and culture it reminds us of how the landscape binds us, in this instance to the textile industry, from the sheep on the moorland uplands to the workers in the mills of the surrounding valleys, we are all to a degree 'interwoven' by the landscape.

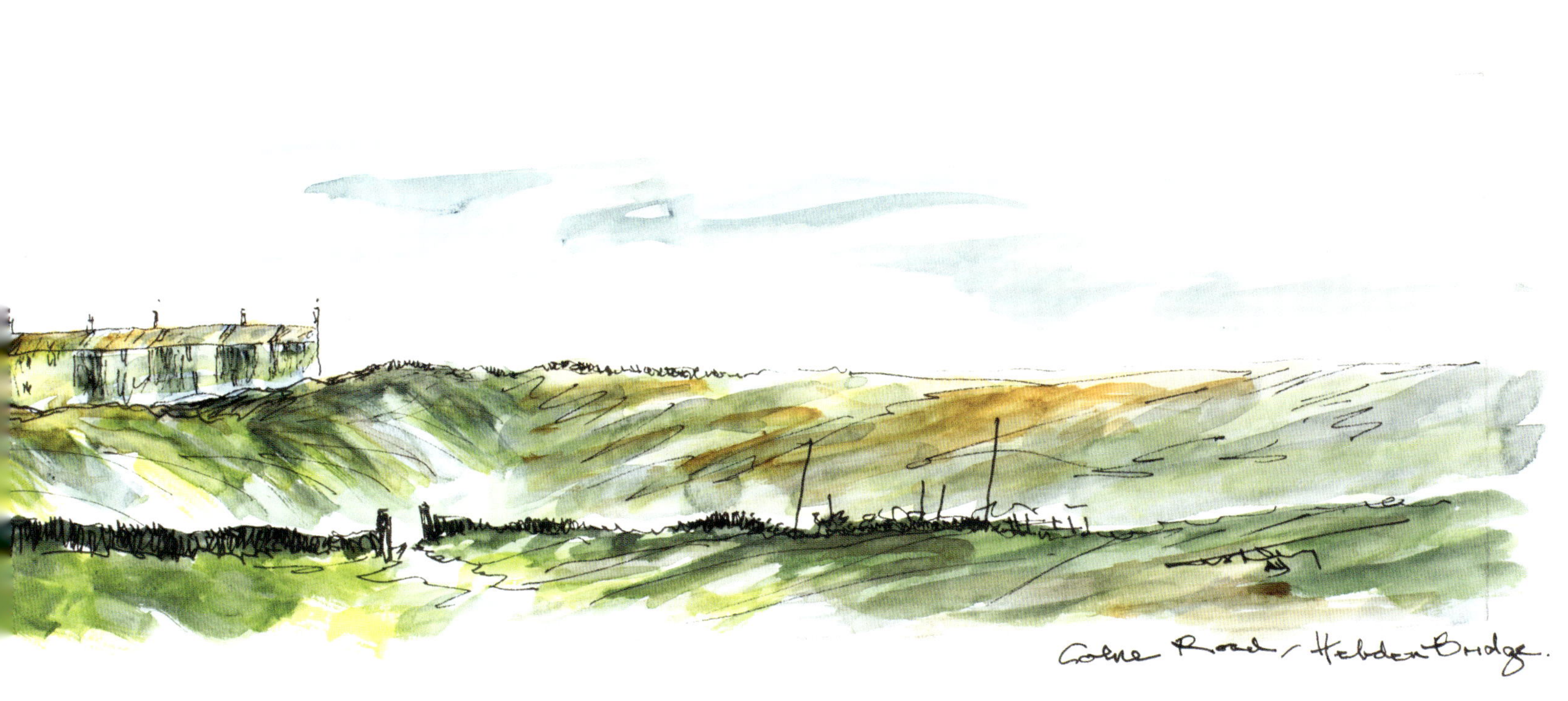

Colne Road, Hebden Bridge.

Looking to Holme Moss from Greenfield Road

Mother nature can assist you if you wish to learn to paint; if you look closely, you will see the colour of the sky reflected in the landscape. If you utilise the same blue of your watercolour for the sky in your mixing of the colours for the landscape, you will find a marriage of landscape and sky. Obviously, like any marriage there are also days of conflict when this will not be true.

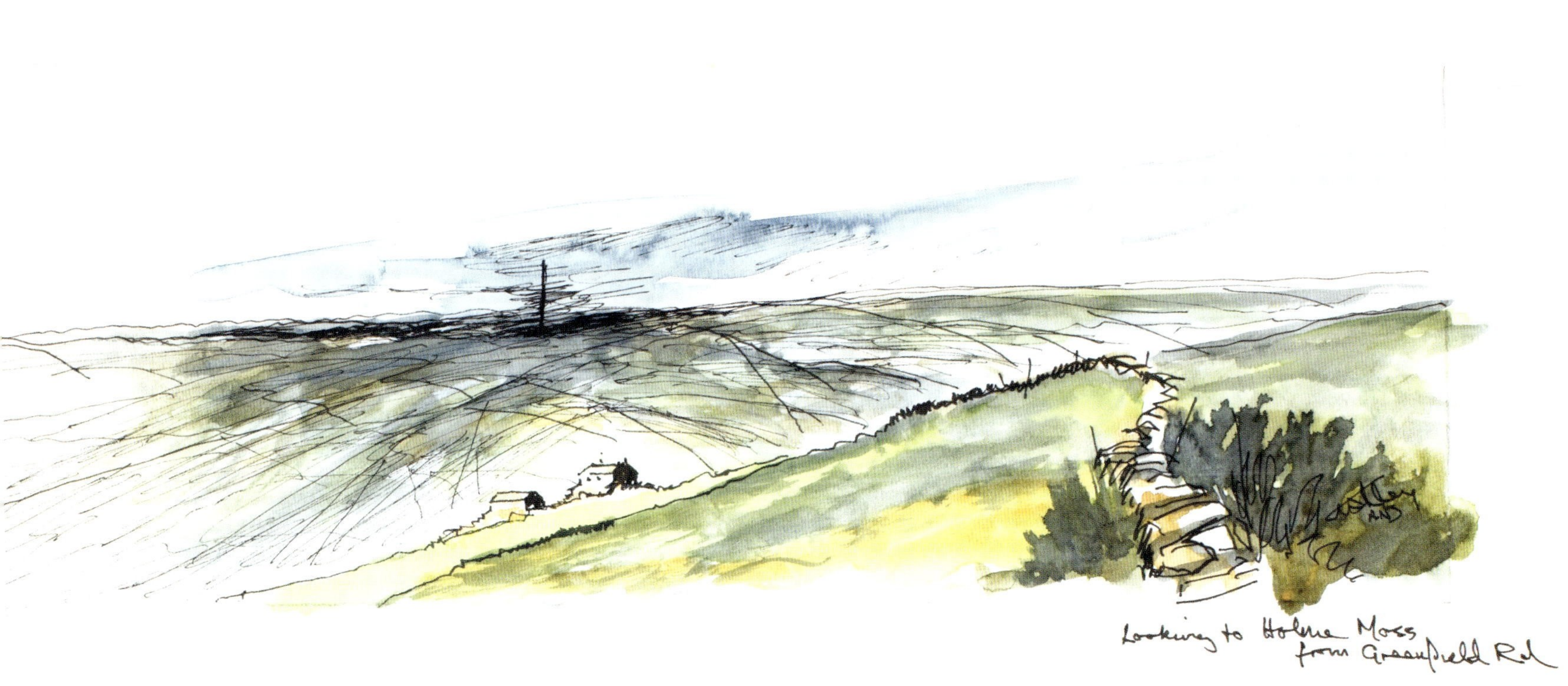

Looking to Holme Moss from Greenfield Road   137

Eskdale, North Yorkshire Moors

When I capture the moorlands of Yorkshire I often compare them to the frozen seas; look closely and you can see the waves rippling out into the distance. I know I am a romantic at heart, why otherwise would I see light on the bleakest of days and see nothing in a day filled with sunshine? I have to believe that when you truly wish to capture a painting, you see with your heart what your eyes do not.

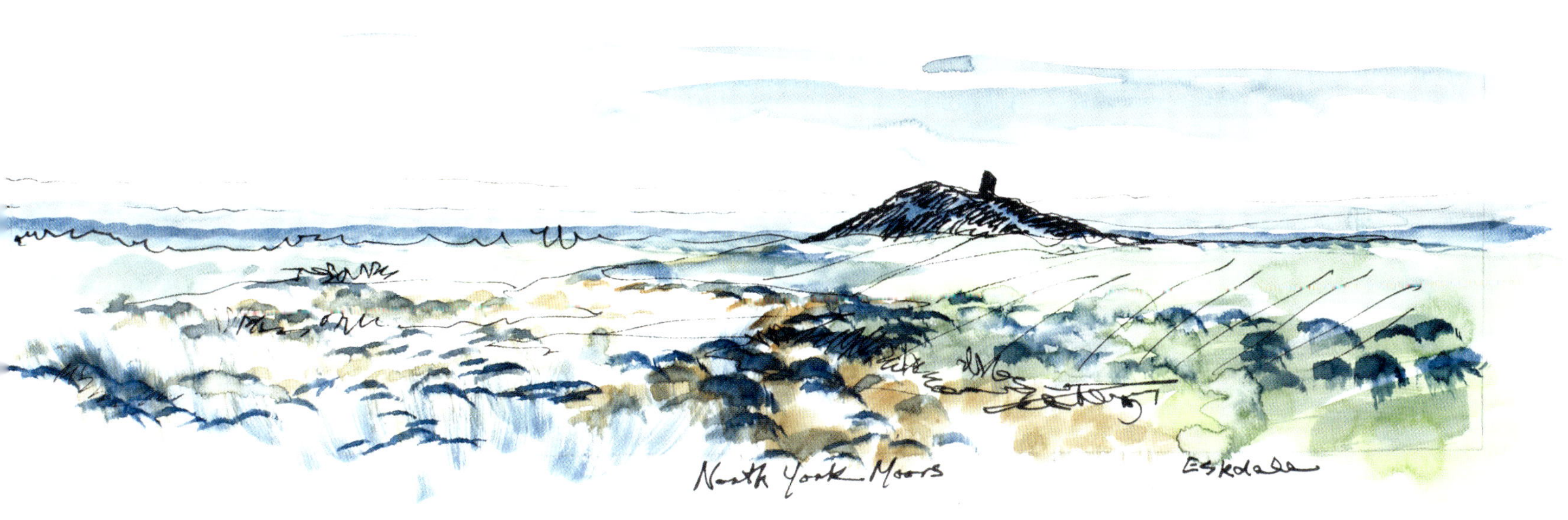

North York Moors
Eskdale

Blackshaw Edge

This was beyond cold when I sketched this; I could feel the chill through my clothes and it seemed to almost seep into my bones. Even the house had an eeriness about it, as if to say don't stay too long. Needless to say I quickly made my sketch and returned to the heat of my car. There is a Methodist church high on Blackshaw Edge and perhaps they built it there on purpose; I think you have to truly believe in something to venture up there on a bitterly cold day.

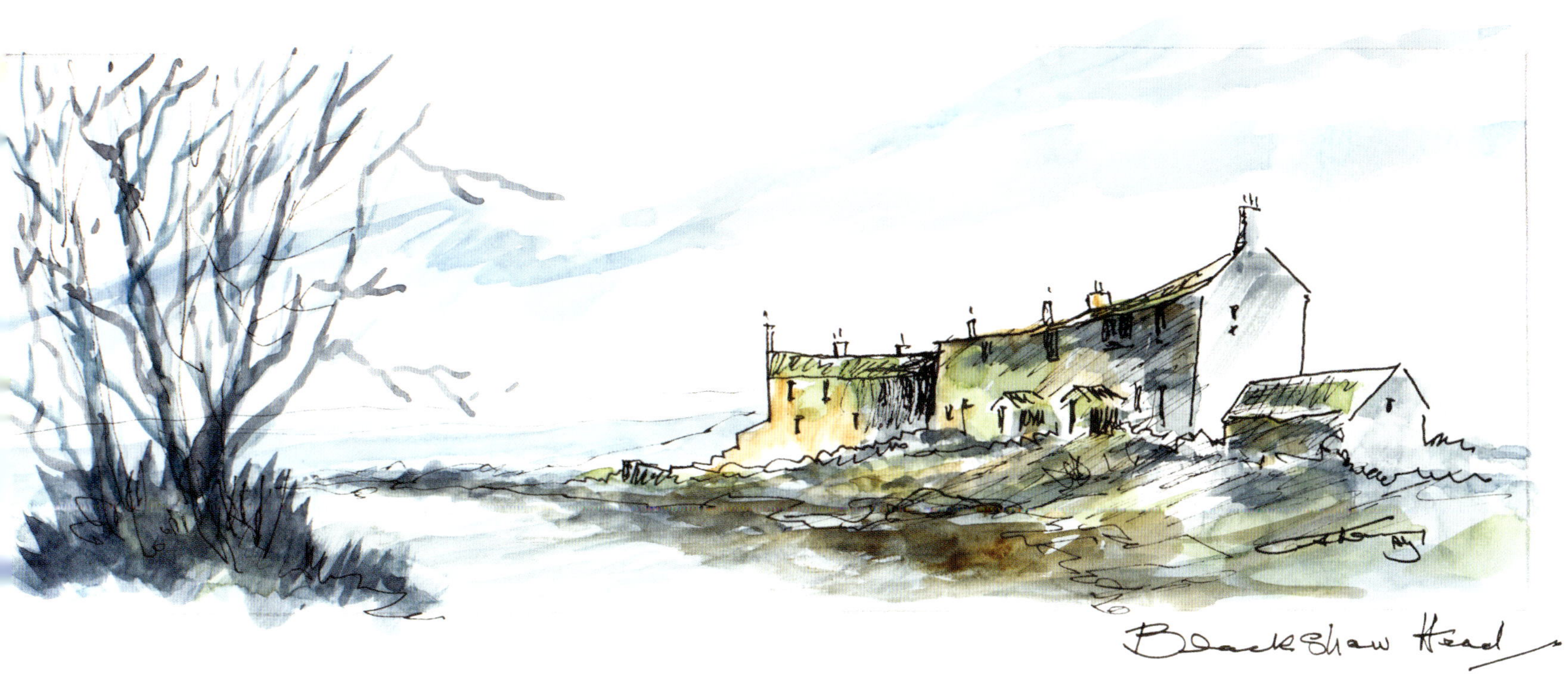

Blackshaw Head

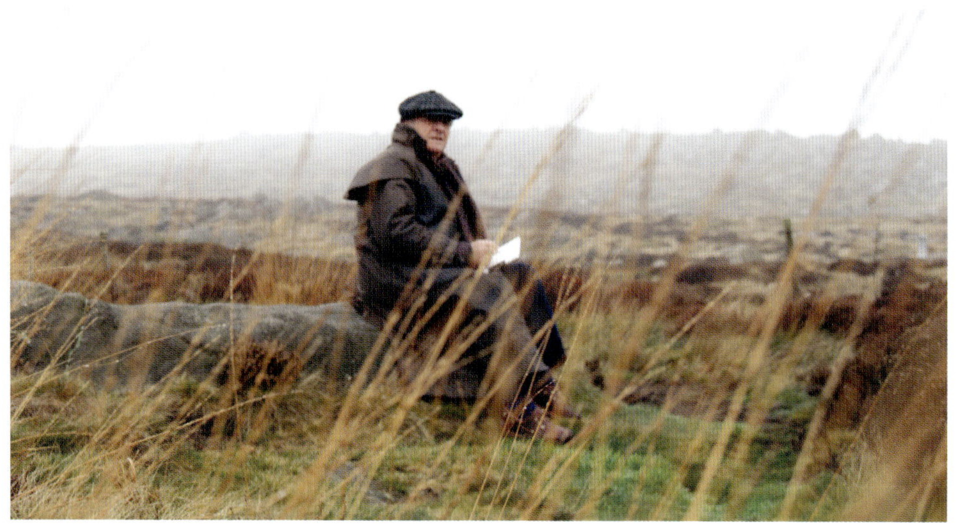

Holme Moss

Yorkshire has really got a strong hold of me.

> *But why should I let her go*
> *And where would I be if she was not there…*
> (Ashley Jackson, 1970)

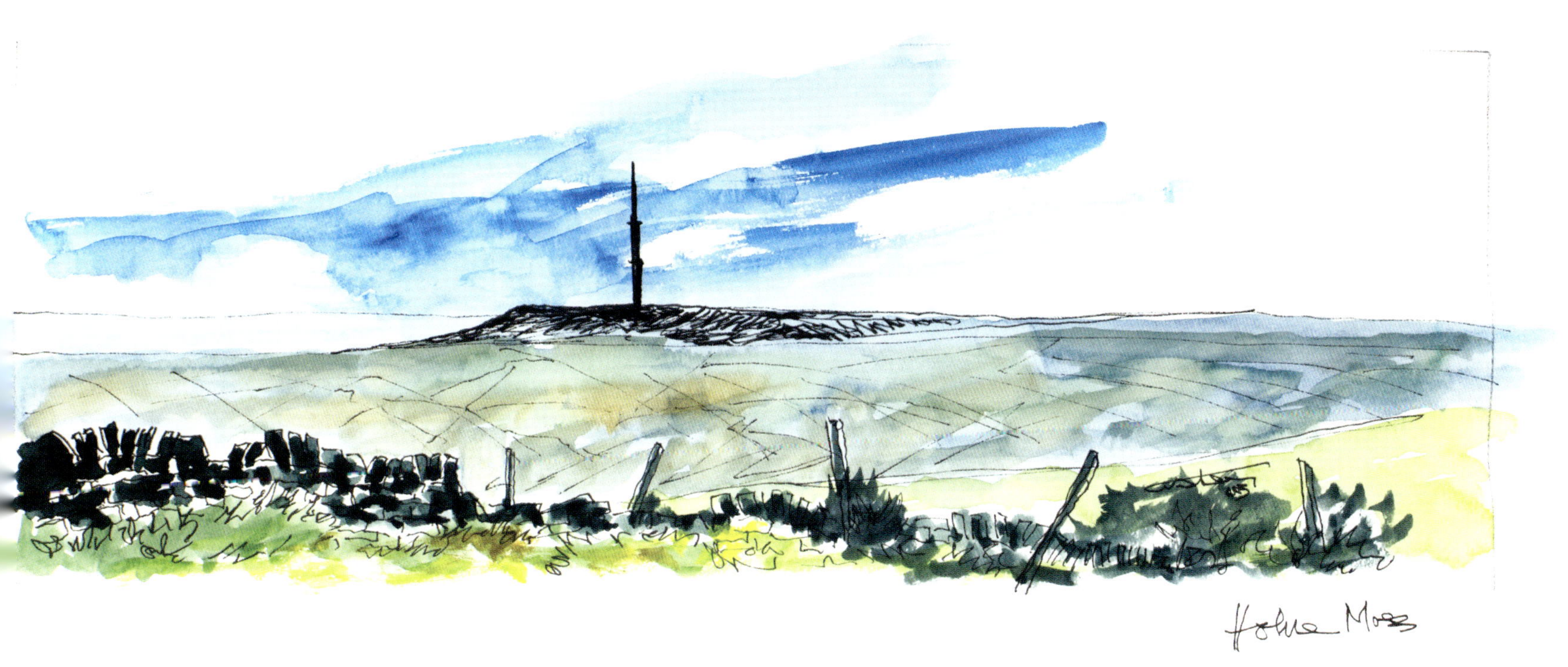

Holme Moss

Final Words

If I can offer one piece of advice from my life in art, it is that just because it doesn't come easily, doesn't mean that art is not for you. You just need to keep practising until you get it right, so that you learn to capture what you see with your eyes, your hands and emotions connecting as one. Life is often about figuring out what you can't do and mastering it.

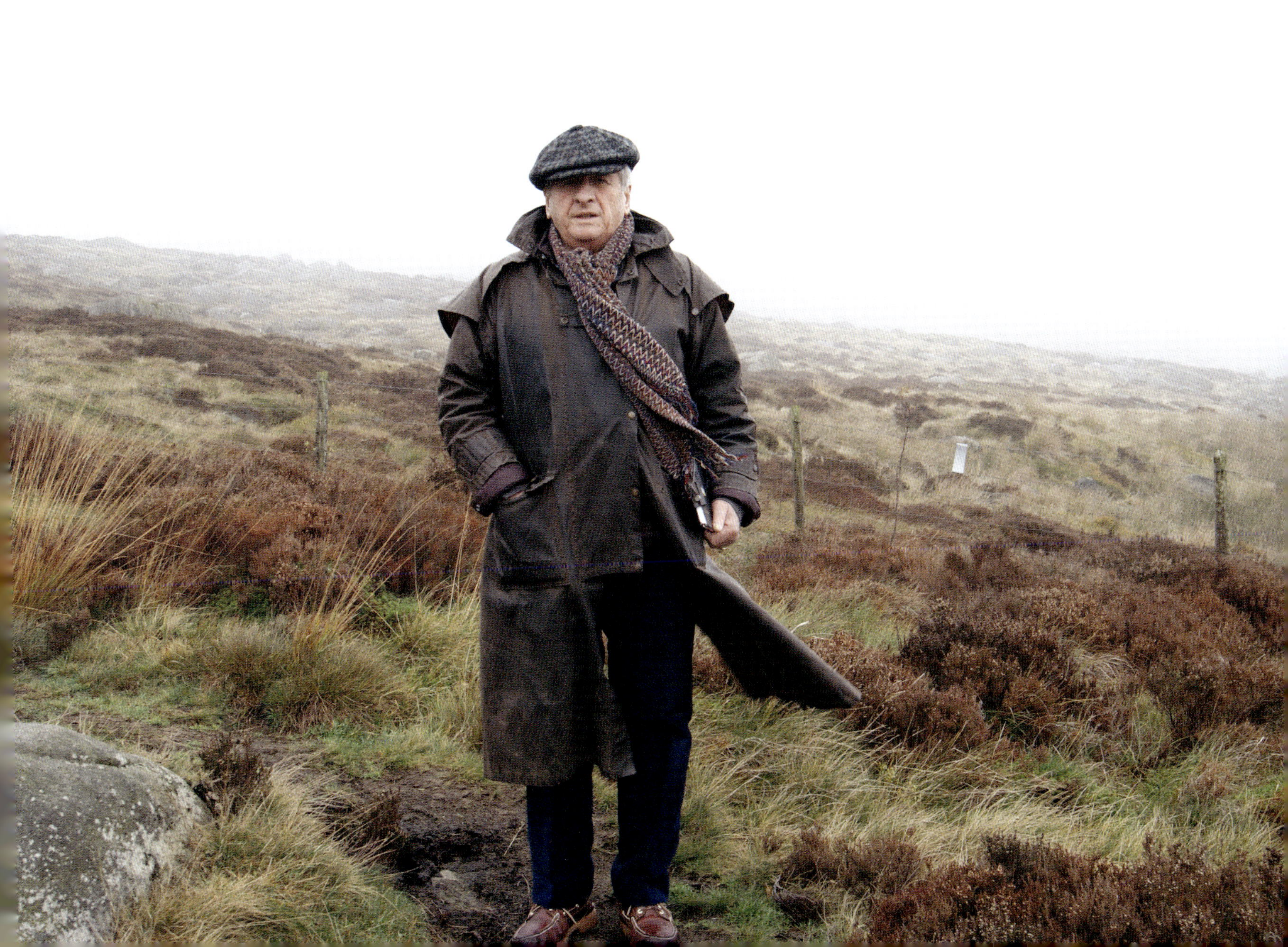

Biography

Since opening his first gallery back in 1963, Ashley Jackson has become one of the country's leading and most successful watercolour artists. He was elected Fellow of the Royal Society of Arts at the age of 26 and has been a professional artist for nearly 60 years. All this time he has chosen to remain committed to the Yorkshire landscape, 'his mistress', and compares their tempestuous relationship to a great love affair.

His paintings have been exhibited worldwide, alongside Picasso and Salvador Dali, and adorn the walls of many successful and famous people, for his art straddles many divisions thanks to the nature of his legacy to make art accessible to all and not just the elite establishment. Art is a great communicator requiring few words to interpret, and as such his television series have been watched by millions over the years, creating an appreciation of not only his atmospheric watercolours, but the landscape which he captures with such deference.

It is this dogmatic persistence that has seen his paintings exhibited in the most unusual settings, with his paintings hanging in locations as varied as NATO headquarters (The Day the World Changed 9/11), to the Grand Central Train named "Ashley Jackson – The Yorkshire Artist" (2010). His work has appeared on the Yorkshire Bank debit card (2008) and even the BT phone book (2003), and it is this aim of making art accessible to all that continues to drive him.

Amongst many awards and accolades, Ashley Jackson was presented with a Hon Doctorate (Uni) by the University of Huddersfield in 2013, for his

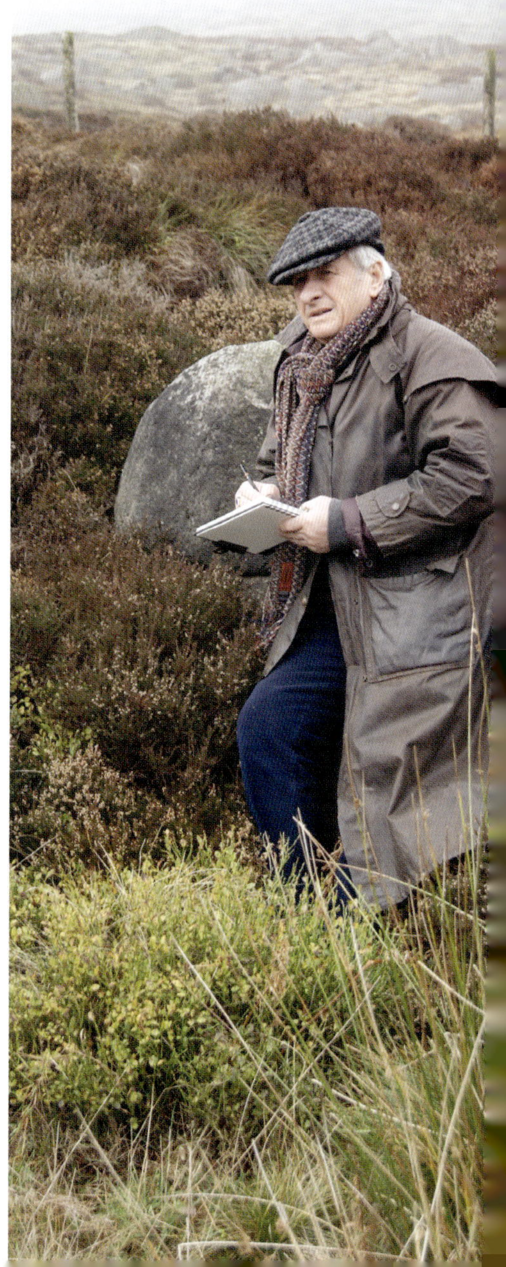

commitment to the Arts; a fantastic accolade bestowed by a committee of his peers, for his dedication to a lifetime's campaign of making art accessible to all. You can view many of his paintings within Student Central at the University.

As he nears his eightieth year he has lost none of his drive not only to encourage people to take up art, but to appreciate the beauty of the landscape around us. It is this commitment that led to Ashley being presented with the British Empire Medal in the Queen's birthday honours of June 2017.

Journalist David Whetstone (*The Journal,* 2008) once wrote on meeting the artist; 'You feel that if Ashley Jackson were cut in half – God forbid – you would find the word "Yorkshire" running through him like a stick of rock'. He is still that man, a little older, with more life experience, but still in love with his Yorkshire Mistress until the day she greets him with a final embrace.

This is but a brief biography, should you wish to find out more about Ashley Jackson there is a biography written by the Features Editor of the *Yorkshire Post,* Chris Bond, called *An Artist's Life*, or visit the website www.ashley-jackson.co.uk.

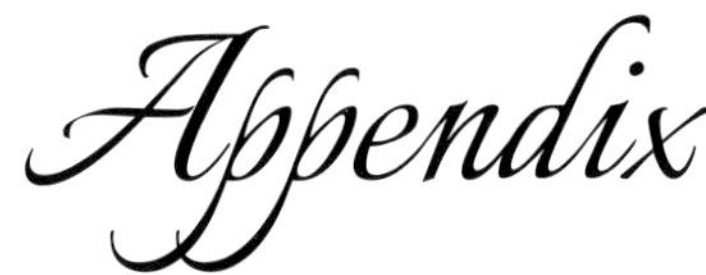

Appendix

One Man Exhibitions

September 2013 – January 2104
"Chasing Light" – The Biscuit Factory, Newcastle.

5 July – 9 August 2013
"Celebrating God's Own County" – Bradford Cathedral.

22 October – 8 May 2010
"Power and the Passion" – previously unseen work celebrating his 70th year, displayed at Temple Newsam House, Leeds.

4 – 9 October 2010
"Power and the Passion" – previously unseen work celebrating his 70th year, displayed at the prestigious Mall Galleries, London.

26 July – 20 October 2008
"Painting in the Open Air" – previously unseen work, displayed at the prestigious Laing Art Gallery, Newcastle.

13 September – 13 October 2003
"Ashley Jackson One Man Exhibition" – Patchings Art Centre, Calverton, Nottinghamshire.

2003

"Ashley Jackson's Yorkshire" – International Yorkshire Business Convention Centre, Yorkshire Showground.

2002

"Ashley Jackson's Yorkshire Moors – A Love Affair" – Victoria Quarter, Leeds.

2002

"The Spirit Never Dies" – Royal Armouries, Leeds.

2000

"Dawn's a New Day" – Royal Armouries, Leeds.

1999

"Twilight of the Twentieth Century" – Cartwright Hall, Bradford.

1997

"Earth, Wind and Fire" – Salford Art Gallery.

1996

"From Yorkshire With Love" – touring exhibition, Beningborough Hall, York; Wakefield Art Gallery; Sewerby Hall, Bridlington.

1995

"Here's to You, Dad" – touring exhibition, Cooper Art Gallery. Barnsley; Smith Gallery, Brighouse; Dewsbury Town Hall; Doncaster Art Gallery.

1994

"My Mistress and I, the Yorkshire Moors" – Rotherham Art Gallery.

1994
Yorkshire Post Headquarters.

1993
Patchings Art Centre – United Society of Artists.

1992
The Coach House Gallery, Lincoln.

1991
"In Harmony with the Moor" – John Worthy Gallery, Leek.
"In Mood with the Moor" – Lauron Gallery, Ilkley.

1990
"My Way, – Art to the People" retrospect exhibition, Huddersfield Art
Gallery, sponsored by Yorkshire Television.

1989
St Louis, U.S.A.

1988
New York, U.S.A.

1987
"Ashley Jackson's Vision of Turner in Yorkshire" – Bass Headquarters,
Huddersfield, opened by H.R.H. Prince of Wales.

1986
"Ashley Jackson's Vision of Turner" – The Mall Galleries, F.B.A., London;
Milan, Italy.

1985
Chicago, New York, Dallas, U.S.A.

1984
Milan, Italy.

1983
The Old Barn, Ruislip.

1982
Washington DC, U.S.A.

1979
Foyles Gallery, London; Maclaurin Art Gallery, Glasgow.

1978
Kidderminster Art Gallery.

1977
Municipal Gallery, Valencia, Spain.

1974
The Mall Gallery, F.B.A., London.

1969
Upper Grosvenor Gallery, West End, London.

1968
Cannon Hall Gallery, Barnsley.
Wakefield Art Gallery.

1967

Brighouse Art Gallery.

1966

Crow Nest Gallery, Dewsbury.

1964

Newark Art Gallery, Nottingham.

1963

Brighouse.

Television Productions

2002

"In a Different Light" – Yorkshire Television.

2001

Ninth series of "A Brush With Ashley" – YTV. New series filming in the Mediterranean.

2000

Eighth series of "A Brush With Ashley"."Some Days are Diamond" – YTV. A half-hour celebratory programme in recognition of Ashley's sixtieth birthday and his contribution to the arts.

1999

Seventh series of "A Brush With Ashley" – YTV. "QE2 B'aht at" – Six part series by YTV featuring Ashley aboard the QE2.

1998
Sixth series of "A Brush With Ashley" – YTV.

1996
Fifth series of "A Brush With Ashley" – YTV.

1995
Fourth series of "A Brush With Ashley" – YTV.

1994
Wire T.V. mini series.

1990 – 1998
"A Brush With Ashley" – TLC (The Learning Channel)

1993
Third series of "A Brush With Ashley" – YTV, Border and Tyne Tees.

1992
Second series of "A Brush With Ashley" – YTV, Border and Tyne Tees.

1990
"A Brush With Ashley" – Yorkshire Tyne Tees & Border Television.

1990
"Profile of an Artist" – BBC Look North.

1984 – 1988
"Ashley Jackson's World of Art" – P.B.S.

1982
"Making the Most of…" – Channel 4.

1981
"Once in a Lifetime – My Own Flesh and Blood" – Network TV.
A documentary on Ashley.

1978 & 1985
Own series on Pebble Mill at One.

1968
Omnibus Programme, BBC.

Books Published

2017
Ashley Jackson: A Lifetime of Inspiration Captured in Watercolour
(Pen & Sword Books)

2012
My Yorkshire Sketchbook (Dalesman)

2010
An Artist's Life by Chris Bond (Pen and Sword Books)

2006
50 Golden Years (Dalesman)

2000
Ashley Jackson's Yorkshire Moors: A love Affair (Dalesman)

1994
Painting the British Isles: A Watercolourist's Journey (Boxtree)

1993

A Brush With Ashley (Boxtree)

1992

Painting in the Open Air (Harper Collins)

1981

My Brush With Fortune (Secker and Warburg)

1981

Ashley Jackson's Worlds of Art, Vols. 1,2 & 3 (Alexander Art Corporation)

1981

An Artist's Notebook

Accolades

1967

Elected Fellow of the Royal Society of Arts. Founder Member of the
Yorkshire Watercolour Society; elected Chairman.

1996

Arts and Entertainment Award – Yorkshire Awards.
Yorkshire Society – Vice Chairman, Vice President.

2004

B.T. selected one of Ashley's paintings to be depicted on the front cover of
the telephone directory.

2005

Freedom of the City of London.

2006

Life Time Achievement Award, Yorkshire Awards.

2007

Life Time Achievement Award, *Huddersfield Examiner.*

2004 – 2009

Ambassador Northern Art.

2008

February Yorkshire Icon Award and Hall of Fame.

2009

Yorkshire Man of the Year, Dalesman Rural Award.

2009

Yorkshire Bank launch debit card with Ashley Jackson painting.

2011

Grand Central name one of their trains "Ashley Jackson – Yorkshire Artist".

2013

Proud to accept Honorary Doctorate from the University of Huddersfield.

2017

Presented with British Empire Medal in the Queen's birthday honours for his contribution to the Arts.

Books:

Entry in *Who's Who in Art*
Debretts' *Distinguished People of Today*

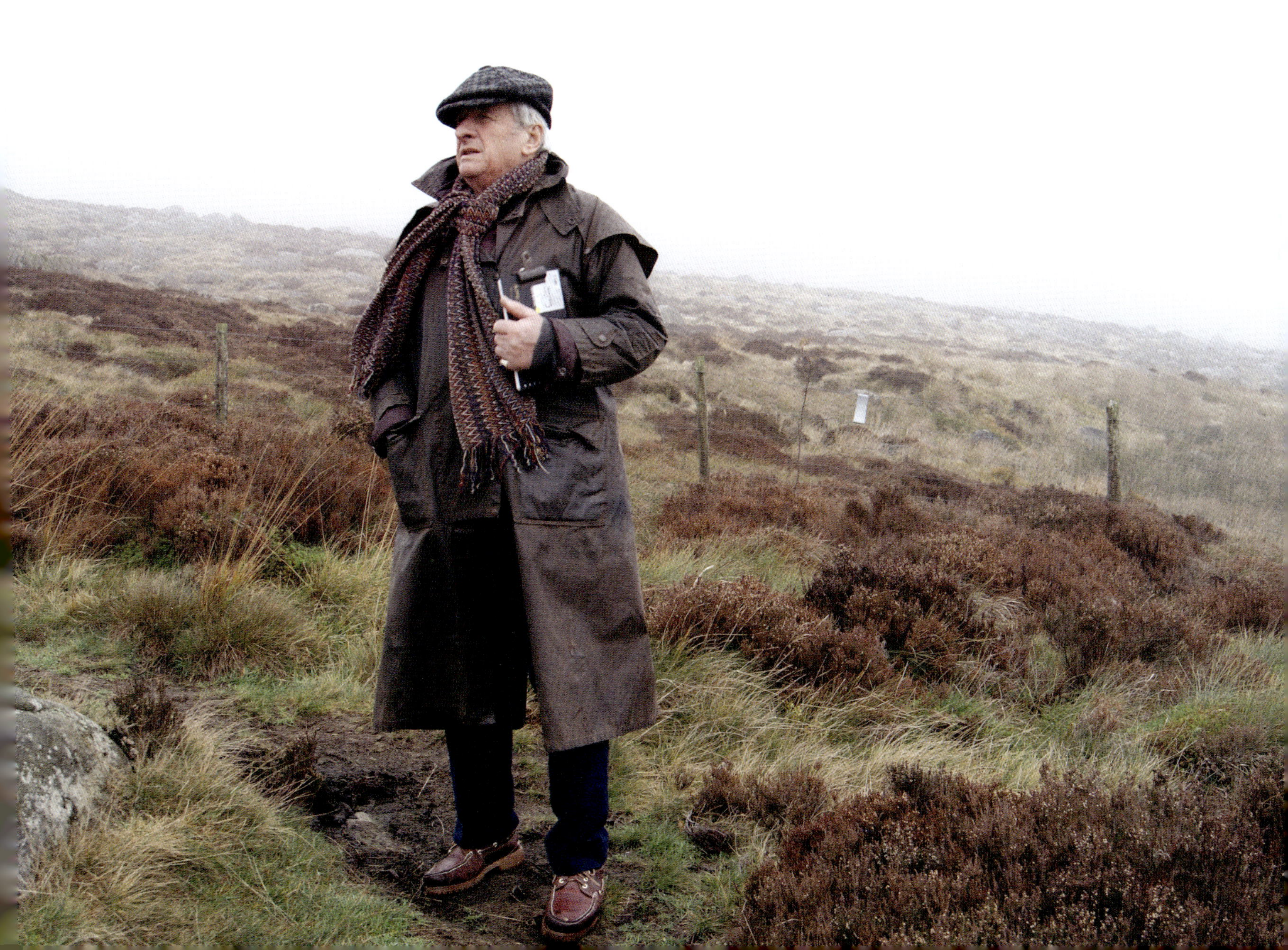

Photographic Credits

Claudia Jackson Berettoni: 9, 10, 11, 38, 39, 46, 76, 116, 128, 142, 145, 146, 157.

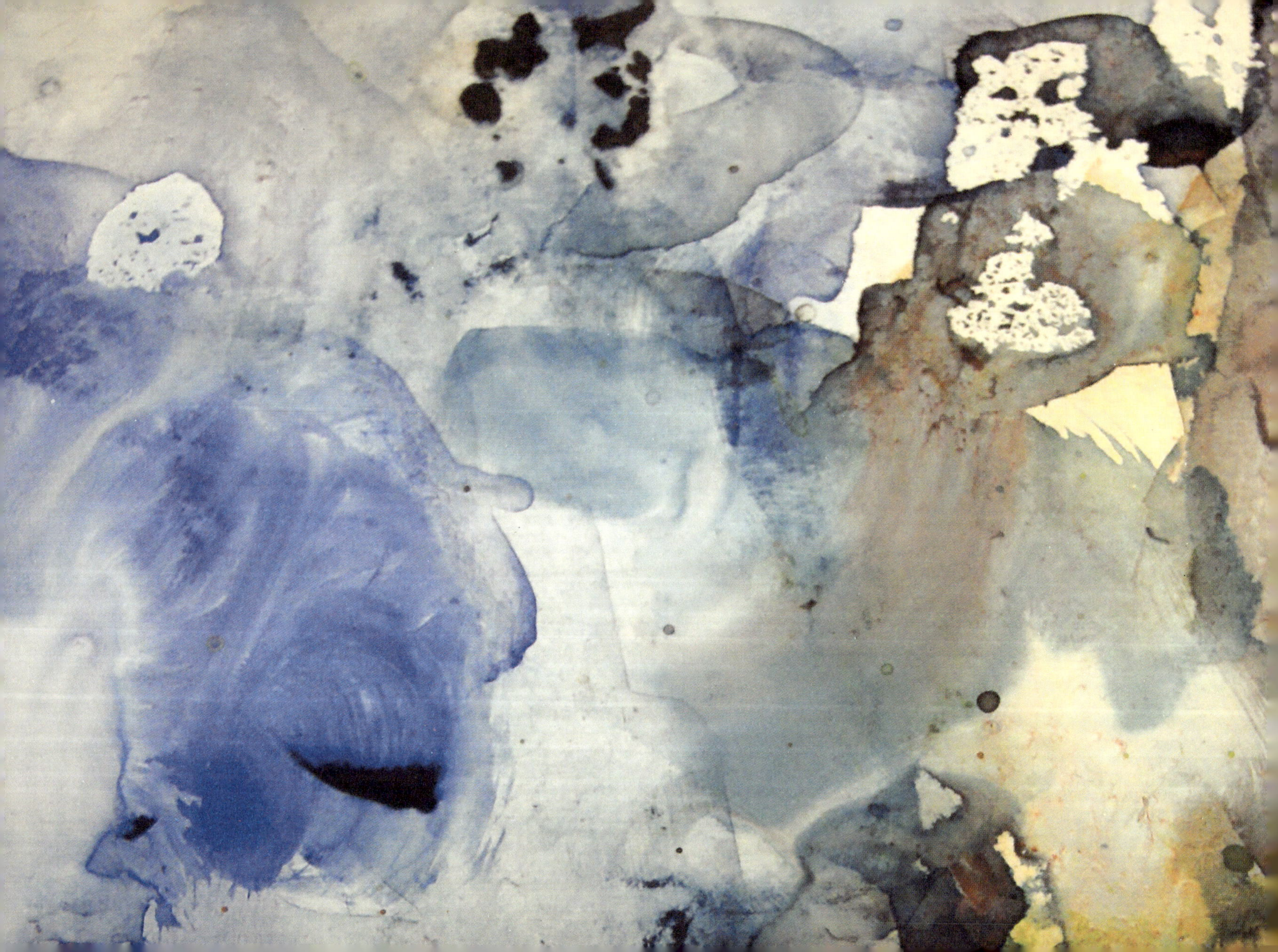